Lecture Notes in Economics and Mathematical Systems

Managing Editors: M. Beckmann and W. Krelle

262

Hans Ulrich Buhl

A Neo-Classical Theory of Distribution and Wealth

Springer-Verlag
Berlin Heidelberg New York Tokyo

Author

Dr. Hans Ulrich Buhl
Institut für Wirtschaftstheorie und Operations Research
Universität Karlsruhe
Kaiserstr. 12, D-7500 Karlsruhe 1, FRG

ISBN 3-540-16062-0 Springer-Verlag Berlin Heidelberg New York Tokyo
ISBN 0-387-16062-0 Springer-Verlag New York Heidelberg Berlin Tokyo

Library of Congress Cataloging-in-Publication Data. Buhl, Hans Ulrich. A neo-classical theory of distribution and wealth. (Lecture notes in economics and mathematical systems; 262) Bibliography: p. 1. Wealth–Mathematical models. 2. Neoclassical school of economics. I. Title. II. Series.
HB251.B85 1986 330'.16 85-30452
ISBN 0-387-16062-0 (U.S.)

Printed in Germany

Printing and binding: Beltz Offsetdruck, Hemsbach/Bergstr.
2142/3140-543210

Acknowledgements

I wish to express my sincere gratitude to Wolfgang Eichhorn for his encouragement and advice during all phases of the research finally leading to this book. My special appreciation also belongs to Andreas Pfingsten and Frank Stehling for stimulating comments and valuable suggestions. In addition, I would like to thank my wife Silvia for her patience and understanding and Ingeborg Kast, Iris Winzrieth, and Matthias Renner for excellent typing of the difficult manuscript.

Table of Contents

1. PREFACE AND INTRODUCTION

The distribution of capital and income in general and its relation to wealth and economic growth in particular have attracted economists' interest for a long time already. Especially the, at least partially, conflicting nature of the two political objectives, namely to obtain substantially large economic growth and a "just" income distribution at the same time, has caused the topic to become a subject of political discussions.

As a result of these discussions, numerous models of workers' participation in the profits of growing economies have been developed. To a minor extent and with quite diverse success, some have been implemented in practice. It is far beyond the scope of this work to outline all these approaches from the past centuries and, in particular, the past decades.

In economic theory many authors, for instance Kaldor [1955], Krelle [1968], [1983], Pasinetti [1962], Samuelson and Modigliani [1966], to name but a few, have analyzed the long-term economic implications of workers' saving and investment. While most of this extensive literature is highly interesting, it suffers from the fact that it does not explicitly consider either workers' or capitalists' objectives and thus neglects their impacts on economic growth. Thus, in the framework of a neo-classical model, these objectives and their impacts will be emphasized here.

A number of authors, briefly surveyed in Chapter 2, have recently succeeded in taking account of these objectives in their models by employing differential games. The only weakpoint of these theories is that quite restrictive economic assumptions are necessary to obtain explicit solutions. Thus, in Chapter 3, the author has decided to employ a different approach. In the model economy considered everything is assumed to be exogeneously given except the workers' or capitalists' control variable and the state of the economic system. One can make fairly general assumptions regarding the economic parameters, the utility functions, and the sequence of production functions. It is still possible to derive optimality conditions and, by imposing some more condition, explicit optimal policies with respect to the objectives considered. By comparing these optimality conditions one may then draw some game-theoretic conclusions.

To elucidate the generality of the results obtained we may, for instance, briefly discuss how technological change is accounted for. By assuming production functions to be constant in time, in most of the earlier models mentioned above technological change was neglected. While this seems appropriate for short-term analysis one may doubt whether or not it is justifiable for long-term economic analysis. The production functions employed here are assumed to depend on capital, labor, and time. Thus, in consecutive periods quite different neo-classical production functions are admissible. No further restrictions are imposed on technological change.[1)]

The way the production functions are formulated, however, only disembodied technological change is allowed for, that is,"technical progress makes new and old capital goods more productive in the same way and in the same proportion" (Solow [1962]). On the other hand, embodied technological change is only incorporated in newly produced capital goods. In Buhl [1983], the author followed Solow's suggestion "to work both sides of the street" and showed how models with disembodied technological change can be modified to account for embodied technological change. Similarly, the results of Chapters 3 and 4 in this work can be modified accordingly.

[1)] If, in consecutive periods, the production functions differ too much, however, no feasible policies may exist. This will be discussed in more detail later.

In Chapter 4, the key results from Chapter 3 are modified for alternative objectives. No proofs or derivations are given there because the results can be obtained similarly as in Chapter 3.

Chapter 5 finally contains a discussion of the economic relevance of the results derived in the preceeding chapters. Most of the theorems from Chapter 3 and the results of Chapter 4 follow from application of the theorems embedded in Chapter 6, a mathematical appendix. Dividing theory and applications into separate chapters has the advantage that economic discussions are not interrupted by theoretical proofs. A list of references in Chapter 7 concludes the book.

2. A SHORT SURVEY

Both, the problem of distribution in an economy as such and the problems of understanding, influencing, and forecasting distribution's implications on economic growth and wealth have been attracting economists for a long time already. For reasons of brevity no attempt will be made to outline the theories of to name but a few Adam Smith, David Ricardo, Thomas R. Maltus, John S. Mill, and Karl Marx.

Kaldor [1955/56] and Pasinetti [1961/62], [1974] later developed mathematical models to determine that distribution between capitalists and workers which is necessary for an economy to remain in full employment equilibrium. In their models they assumed the saving behavior of both groups to be exogeneously specified and to be constant in time. Thus each distribution uniquely determines a certain investment in each period and a certain economic growth path.

The models of Kaldor and Pasinetti later were challenged and generalized by Modigliani/Samuelson [1966], Tobin [1963], and Meade [1963].

The partially complementary and partially conflicting nature of capitalists' and workers' objectives influencing investment, saving behavior, and thus economic growth, however, are not addressed in these models. Since the present work emphasizes the formulation of optimal policies for both groups, they will not be discussed further.

Based on the work of Kaldor and Pasinetti, Vellupillai [1982] developed a model to analyze the dynamics of workers' saving and investment. Although Vellupillai points to the different objectives of both groups, he does not make these objectives explicit but only makes behavioral assumptions in the model equations. At the end of his paper he suggests: "An even more important, and perhaps more interesting, direction in which to proceed, would be to make more explicit the nature of the conflicting and complementary nature of the relationship between capital and labour. The most elegant way, within the framework of dynamical systems, would be to use differential games."

2.1 LANCASTER'S MODEL

With a very simple model, this approach was chosen by Lancaster [1973]. Lancaster assumes a technology with a fixed output/capital ratio a; thus letting K(t) denote the capital stock and Y(t) total output at time t, we have a linear production function of K(t):

$$(2.1)\qquad Y(t) = aK(t), \quad a>0, \quad t\geqq 0.$$

Lancaster argues "that the workers do have some limited control over one of the key variables, the ratio of worker consumption to total output" exercised by

- bargaining power,
- saving[1],
- electoral politics.

In his model, Lancaster gives the workers full control, to "determine, between given upper and lower limits, the ratio of current worker consumption to total output", i.e.,

$$(2.2)\qquad u^w(t) = C^w(t)/Y(t), \quad t\geqq 0$$

at each instant of time, where

$$0<c \leqq u^w(t) \leqq b<1, \; b>1/2.$$

---

[1] Lancaster interprets workers' saving as "voluntarily handing over part of their income in the hope or belief (...) that the capitalists will use it for true capital investment...".

Letting investment be denoted by $I(t)$ and capitalists consumption by $C^c(t)$, Lancaster assumes the "capitalists can determine what proportion of that output not consumed by workers is to be invested and what proportion to be devoted to their own consumption"

$$u^c(t) = I(t)/(Y(t)-C^w(t)),$$

$$(2.3) \quad 1-u^c(t) = C^c(t)/(Y(t)-C^w(t)),$$

$$0 \leqq u^c(t) \leqq 1, \quad t \geqq 0.$$

The objectives of both, workers and capitalists, are to maximize their respective total consumption over a fixed time interval [0,T], where T is assumed to be sufficiently large to guarantee that investment pays off at least at time t=0. Since "workers can manipulate u^w but not u^c and capitalists can manipulate u^c but not u^w", "this is a very simple differential game". (Lancaster [1973,p.1098]).

Solving this game via Pontryagin's maximum principle, Lancaster shows the model's solution to be bang-bang, which, by the linearity of equation (2.1) is certainly not very surprising. The switching point is determined to be

$$(2.4) \quad \bar{t} = T - \frac{1}{a(1-b)},$$

and the solution consists of two phases:

(i) In the time interval $[0,\bar{t})$ workers and capitalists consume minimally; thus we have maximum investment up to time $\bar{t}$.

(ii) In the interval $[\bar{t},T]$ both groups consume maximally and investment is equal to zero.

Comparing the solution of the non-cooperative differential game with the solution of the cooperative game, where total consumption is maximized, Lancaster finds the switching point of the latter

$$(2.5) \quad t^* = T - \frac{1}{a}$$

to be later than $\bar{t}$ because of $0<b<1$. Then Lancaster continues and shows that total consumption of the cooperative game C^* is strictly larger than total consumption of the non-cooperative game $\bar{C} = C^w+C^c$. It is this difference what Lancaster calls "the dynamic inefficiency of capitalism". This dynamic inefficiency holds for all finite horizons T. It results, "of course, from the failure of the system to accumulate during the interval $[\bar{t},t^*)$" (Lancaster [1973,p.1105]). We remark, however, that in the interval $[0,\bar{t})$ "capitalist accumulation" is equivalent to the social optimum. Since economies usually are not designed to end at some time T, Lancaster's result does not directly describe an observable phenomenon but is thus far mainly of theoretical interest.

2.2 HOEL'S MODELS

Hoel [1978] generalizes Lancaster's model by introducing concave and strictly increasing utility functions for both, workers and capitalists. Both groups' objective is assumed to be maximizing the present value of utility instead of maximizing total consumption only.

Again, the time horizon T is assumed to be sufficiently large to guarantee that investment pays off at least at time $t = 0$. Hoel then shows, that the non-cooperative game solution "cannot be Pareto optimal, as there exist feasible solutions which give both workers and capitalists a higher welfare level" (see Hoel [1978,pp.337]).

A necessary condition for such a game solution to be Pareto optimal would be that the above assumption of the time horizon is not satisfied and we thus have zero investment in the whole interval [O,T]. Hoel also shows in his paper, "there exist cases where all of the Pareto optimal solutions have higher accumulation than the game solution, as well as cases where at least one Pareto optimal solution has a lower accumulation than the game solution". For more detail, interesting and thorough investigations and interpretations as well as an infinite horizon generalization of Lancaster's model, see Hoel [1975,pp.57].

2.3 POHJOLA'S MODELS

Various relevant extensions of Lancaster's model framework were conducted by Pohjola [1983a] [1983b] [1983c] [1984a] [1984b]. In his [1983b] paper Pohjola takes Lancaster's open-loop Nash equilibrium as a reference solution, derives the corresponding open-loop Stackelberg solutions under both workers' and capitalists' leadership, and finally compares the Stackelberg games with the Nash game. He shows the Stackelberg game with the workers as leaders and the capitalists as followers to consist of three phases. In the second phase, workers consume minimally while capitalists have stopped investing and consume maximally. In the first and third phase, both groups behave as in Lancaster's game in the first and second phase. If the capitalists assume leadership in the Stackelberg game, however, the solution again consists of the two phases from Lancaster's game. Under the assumption $b+c>1$ the switch takes place at

$$t' = T - \frac{1}{a(1-c)} .$$

Pohjola shows that both groups prefer the Stackelberg game to the Nash game and that the Stackelberg game is in a stalemate: neither group wants to act as the leader because both prefer to be the follower. He interprets this result as an explanation for the workers' reluctance in some countries to reveal their strategy first.

In a later differential game analysis of threats and bargaining in capitalism, Pohjola [1983b] first derives optimal threats for both social classes. He then shows that due to the capitalists' direct control over capital accumulation "their bargaining power is greater than the workers'."

In two subsequent papers [1984a] and [1984b] Pohjola seeks for explanations of the commonly observed phenomena of high real wages, slow growth, and unemployment. By determining the open-loop Nash equilibrium of a nonzero-sum n-player differential game, he shows in his [1984a] paper, that the trade unions wage rivalry may be an explanation for the observed phenomena. "The lack of power over others' (unions) actions leads each trade union to set the real wage rate of its members at the highest level earlier than all unions would collectively do". The larger the number of trade unions is, the larger is the dynamic welfare loss resulting from the noncooperative situation.

In his paper [1984b], Pohjola gives up the assumptions of a finite planning horizon and the linear utility functions of both social groups. Instead, he introduces logarithmic utility functions and works with an infinite planning horizon. Assuming a labor-surplus economy in which, again, the production function is linear in K, Pohjola shows that the dynamic welfare loss is also preserved in this model framework. As compared to the cooperative solution, in the noncooperative one the wage rate is higher and the growth rates of capital, output, and employment are smaller. Pohjola interprets all these results as an explanation for the phenomena mentioned above which are observable in many economies.

Note, that both in Lancaster's and in Hoel's models as well as in Pohjola's models discussed so far the workers were not assumed to have any control over investment whatsoever.
One reason for the "dynamic inefficiency of capitalism" cer-

tainly was, that the workers could only hope but never know whether the capitalists would use their saving for true investment. Based on this observation and to analyze the economic implications of workers' investment funds, Pohjola [1983a] examined the effects of such a partial transfer of control from capitalists to workers in Lancaster's model framework. We will describe this approach in more detail. Just as Lancaster, Pohjola assumes that both groups are maximizing their own undiscounted consumption in the time interval [0,T], where T is again assumed large enough to guarantee positive saving and investment at least in t = 0. Contrary to Lancaster, however, Pohjola assumes that "the workers can decide whether their savings will be invested or not" (Pohjola [1983a,p.272]). Thus, he lets the workers control the shares or their consumption and investment in the total output, i.e.,

$$\begin{aligned} u_1^w(t) &= C^w(t)/Y(t), \\ u_2^w(t) &= I^w(t)/Y(t), \end{aligned} \tag{2.6}$$

where

$$0<c \leqq u_1^w(t) \leqq u_1^w(t)+u_2^w(t) = b<1,$$
$$b>\frac{1}{2}, \quad t\geqq 0.$$

In Pohjola's model, the capitalists control the share of their investment in output which is not consumed or invested by the workers, i.e.,

$$u^c(t) = I^c(t)/(Y(t)-C^w(t)-I^w(t)), \tag{2.7}$$

where

$$0 \leqq u^c(t) \leqq 1, \quad t\geqq 0.$$

By determining the non-cooperative open-loop Nash equilibrium of his game, Pohjola obtains the switching points

$$(2.8)\qquad \hat{t} = T - \frac{1}{ab} - \frac{\ln[b(1-c)/(1-b)(2b-c)]}{a(b-c)} ,$$

$$(2.9)\qquad \tilde{t} = T - \frac{1}{ab}$$

and the optimal solution consists of three phases:

(i) In the time interval $[0,\hat{t})$ both groups consume minimally and invest maximally.

(ii) In $[\hat{t},\tilde{t})$ the workers still accumulate at the maximum rate, while the capitalists are consuming their share of output.

(iii) In $[\tilde{t},T]$ both groups consume maximally such that investment has fallen to zero.

At first glance it is surprising that the capitalists stop investing before the workers do so. The reason for that, however, simply lies in the assumption that the workers' share in output is larger than the capitalists' one. Because workers can be sure that their savings are invested and, moreover, are invested as productively as capitalists' investment, the assumption $b>1/2$ makes workers' investment pay off also in the time interval $[\hat{t},\tilde{t})$ where capitalists' investment do not.

The optimal solution of the cooperative game is, as we know from Lancaster's game, maximum investment up to t^* from formula (2.5) and maximum consumption thereafter . It is easy to show that[1)]

$$(2.10)\qquad t^* > \tilde{t} > \hat{t} > \bar{t}$$

and that both groups consumption is larger when the switching

---

1) $\tilde{t}>\hat{t}$ because of $z=b(1-c)/(1-b)(2b-c)>1$ and $\hat{t}>\bar{t}$ because of $z-1-\ln z>0$ for $z>1$.

points are closer to t*. Thus, just as in Lancaster's game, a dynamic welfare loss also holds for Pohjola's game but it is strictly smaller in the latter. Note that in the latter both, workers and capitalists, are investing for a longer time than in Lancaster's game. The workers do so because now they can be sure that their savings are actually invested, as mentioned above already. And the capitalists do so, because they know that the workers are investing for a longer time. We thus conclude that the reduction in the dynamic welfare loss is due to taking away one conflict from the non-cooperative situation. Therefore we came closer to the cooperative situation but did not quite reach it.

2.4 MACHACZEK'S MODEL

Notice, that in all the game-theoretic models considered so far quite simple and questionable assumptions about the distributive shares in output were made. The workers could decide about their share bY(t) in output and the capitalists about the rest. Questionable is in particular, that this share does not depend at all on workers' saving and investment behavior. For instance, in Pohjola's model workers invest maximally in the time interval $[\hat{t},\tilde{t})$, while capitalists invest nothing. Why then should workers'share remain constant in time, anyway? Clearly, for taking care of such problems, the question of ownership of workers' saving or investment cannot be neglected any more.

In his model, Machaczek [1984] takes this into account and distinguishes between workers' and capitalists' capital stocks $K^w(t)$ and $K^c(t)$, respectively. To motivate his approach, he cites Pasinetti criticizing the Kaldorian models (Machaczek [1984,p.93]). *"There is a logical slip in the theory... . The authors have neglected the important fact, that, in any type of society, when any individual saves a part of his income, he must also be allowed to own it, otherwise he would not save at all. This means that the stock of capital which exists in the system is owned by those people (capitalists or workers) who in the past made the corresponding savings. ... Therefore total profits themselves must be divided into two categories: profits which accrue to the capitalists and profits which accrue to the workers.".*

He assumes, that wages constitute a constant proportion of output, i.e.,

$$(2.11) \qquad W(t) = b\,Y(t), \quad \tfrac{1}{2}<b<1,$$

but profits are distributed between workers and capitalists according to capital ownership, i.e.,

$$(2.12) \qquad \begin{aligned} P^W(t) &= \frac{K^W(t)}{K^W(t)+K^C(t)}(1-b)Y(t), \\ P^C(t) &= \frac{K^C(t)}{K^W(t)+K^C(t)}(1-b)Y(t). \end{aligned}$$

The objectives of both groups and the production assumptions are left unchanged, and the workers control the share of their total income to be invested, i.e.,

$$(2.13) \qquad I^W(t) = u^W(t)[W(t)+P^W(t)],$$

where

$$0 \leqq u^W(t) \leqq c \leqq 1, \quad 0 \leqq c \leqq 1.$$

The capitalists control the share of their profits to be reinvested, i.e.,

$$(2.14) \qquad I^C(t) = u^C(t)P^C(t), \quad 0 \leqq u^C(t) \leqq 1.$$

Machaczek shows the optimal solution of his game to consist, again, of three phases:

(i) In the time interval $[0,\bar{t})$ both groups consume at minimum and invest at maximum rate.

(ii) In $[\bar{t},t^*)$ the workers keep investing maximally while the capitalists have stopped to invest and consume all their profits.

(iii) In $[t^*,T]$ both groups consume all their income, just as in the optimal solution of the cooperative game.

Recall that $\bar{t} = T-1/a(1-b)$ was the switching point in Lancaster's game, while $t^*= T-1/a$ was the switching point of the cooperative game. Thus, the workers behave optimally in the sense of the cooperative situation and the capitalists behave just like in Lancaster's game.

At first glance, this result seems, again, surprising. Note, however, that the workers obtain all the reward from their investment, wages and profits. Thus, with respect to their investment they are not in a game type situation with the capitalists as players. Both groups' investments are, by the linearity of technology (2.1), completely independent of each other. This explains, why in this game we obtain for the workers the same policy as in the cooperative situation.

The capitalists, on the other hand, behave different because they only obtain the profits but not the wages resulting from their investment. Thus, they stop investing sooner and at the same time as in Lancaster's game because their situation has not changed at all.

By taking away some conflict from the non-cooperative situation, we again have obtained a result closer to the cooperative situation.

The following table sums up the main results of the Nash differential games that have been thoroughly discussed so far:

Let $T>1/a(1-b)$. Then we have the following switching points for Lancaster's, Pohjola's [1983a] and Machaczek's [1984] games:

$$t^* = T-1/a, \qquad \tilde{t} = T-1/ab$$

$$\hat{t} = T-\frac{1}{ab}-\frac{\ln[(b-c)/(1-b)(2b-c)]}{a(b-c)}$$

$$\bar{t} = T-1/a(1-b)$$

and it holds

$$t^* > \tilde{t} > \hat{t} > \bar{t}.$$

Main Results Different phases	Cooperative Game/Policy	Lancaster [1973]	Pohjola [1983a]	Machaczek [1984]
I both groups invest at maximum rate	$[0,t^*)$	$[0,\bar{t})$	$[0,\hat{t})$	$[0,\bar{t})$
II workers save maximally, capitalists consume maximally	-	-	$[\hat{t},\tilde{t})$	$[\bar{t},t^*)$
III both groups consume maximally	$[t^*,T]$	$[\bar{t},T]$	$[\tilde{t},T]$	$[t^*,T]$

Table 2.15

2.5 BÜRK'S MODELS

After an extensive investigation of solution concepts for both, non-cooperative and cooperative n-player games, Bürk [1976] applies his results to the two-player-distribution game between workers and capitalists discussed before.

Contrary to all the models described so far, Bürk does not assume a linear technology (2.1) but rather works with a linear homogeneous Cobb-Douglas production function. Both groups are also being assumed to maximize consumption. However, Bürk neither uses an utility function nor discounting. With a somewhat different interpretation, he also gives the workers the power to control (within certain limits) their consumption rate, while the capitalists can allocate the remaining output to consumption or investment.

Bürk then derives the optimal open-loop Nash solution of the non-cooperative game and shows it to be unique. After an extensive sensitivity analysis he also investigates the cooperative case.

Finally comparing the solution concepts, he shows that neither the Maxmin nor the Nash solutions are Pareto optimal, if the economy does not start up with a very large capital stock already. In this case, the overall optimal saving rate is equal to zero. Note that these results check with the ones from Hoel, [1975] and [1978], discussed before. Using a modification of the overtaking criterion from Weizsäcker [1965], Bürk concludes his analysis with an investigation of the infinite planning horizon case.

2.6 SUMMARY AND DISCUSSION OF SOME LIMITATIONS

A common result of all the differential game models set up to analyze distribution and growth is the following: The game type situation between workers and capitalists will usually lead to what Lancaster called the dynamic welfare loss resulting from the separation of the saving and the investment decision.

Only under very special assumptions, e.g. a very short planning horizon T or a very large initial capital stock K_0 the non-cooperative game yields the same consumption path for the whole economy as the cooperative one. Since it is well known in game theory that such an identity only holds under very restrictive conditions, this result is certainly not very surprising. Thus, the result of the dynamic welfare loss mainly stems from the assumed game type situation and not from other features of the models.

Nevertheless the models prove that the non-cooperative game element, certainly at least partially given in reality, will usually bring about inefficiency if there are no other mechanisms driving the systems towards the cooperative solution.

Obvious limitations of the models discussed mainly are due to their extreme simplicity. Most authors assumed a linear technology (2.1), only Bürk [1976] worked with a Cobb-Douglas production function. Technological change as well as variations of the exogeneous model parameters are excluded from the analysis. Of course, as many authors argue, the simplicity of the models has the definitive advantage of allowing to derive explicit solutions, which usually cannot be obtained in more realistic and therefore more complicated differential game models.

Looking at the results, we find another limitation in the solutions being of the bang-bang type. In the models of Lancaster, Pohjola, and Machaczek we generally obtained such solutions and derived the inefficiency or dynamic welfare loss by comparing such bang-bang solutions. Since these, however, give no guidance for practical applications and do not describe observable phenomena, the model approach is certainly questionable.

Another limitation is the sole examination of 2-player-games. If it is agreed that the game type situation holds for most economies, we definitly should account for more than two conflicting groups in the economy. On the other hand this simplification is certainly justifiable because <u>one</u> important conflict situation common to most economies is indeed caught in these models.

For a discussion of more limitations and prospects for further research, we point to the original papers.

3. A DISCRETE MODEL OF DISTRIBUTION AND WEALTH

In this chapter, we will formulate a discrete economic model to analyze the relationships between distribution and wealth. As in the models outlined in the preceding chapter, we distinguish between two groups in the society, workers and capitalists. With respect to both groups' objectives, optimal strategies will be derived and analyzed, how these compare in the non-cooperative and in the cooperative case.

The model economy is characterized by the following assumptions.

(A1) *Production*

Let K_t denote the value of the economy's capital stock and L_t the number of workers employed in period t, $t = 1,2,\ldots$. The Gross National Product (GNP) in period t, Y_t is a non-decreasing function $F: \mathbb{R}_+^2 \times \mathbb{N} \rightarrow \mathbb{R}_+$ [1] depending on capital K_{t-1}, labor L_{t-1} and time t, i.e.,

$$(3.1)\quad Y_t = F(K_{t-1}, L_{t-1}, t),\ t = 1,2,\ldots .$$

Thus, technology depends exogenously and solely on time t. The non-decreasing production function, with respect to capital and labor, is assumed to be concave, continuously differentiable twice, and linerarly homogeneous. In each period t, capital is depreciated with rate $m_t \in [0,1]$.

1) $\mathbb{R}$, $\mathbb{R}_+$, $\mathbb{R}_{++}$ are the sets of all, nonnegative, strictly positive real numbers; since part-time employment is allowed for, L_t is a continuous variable.

(A2) *Distribution*

In period t each worker employed receives the same wage w_{t-1} for his work in the preceding period t-1. Thus, total wages in the economy are given by

$$(3.2)\quad W_t = w_{t-1}L_{t-1} \ , \qquad t = 1,2,\ldots\ .^{1)}$$

Similarly, when d_t denotes average dividend payment per worker employed, total dividends payed to the workers for their saving and investment are in period t

$$(3.3)\quad D_t = d_{t-1}L_{t-1} \ , \qquad t = 1,2,\ldots\ .$$

Thus, at time t the capitalists receive the residual

$$(3.4)\quad R_t = F(K_{t-1}, L_{t-1}, t) - W_t - D_t \ , \quad t = 1,2,\ldots\ .$$

(A3) *Saving and Investment*

The workers save and invest in period t of their wage income the fraction $a_t^w \in [0,1]$ and also the fraction $a_t^d \in [0,1]$ of their dividendincome. The capitalists invest the fraction $u_t \in [0,1]$ of their residual R_t at time t. Thus, total gross investment in period t is given by

$$(3.5)\quad I_t^g = a_t^w W_t + a_t^d D_t + u_t R_t \ , \qquad t = 1,2,\ldots\ .$$

---

1) In most of the following analysis, w_t may also be interpreted as the average wage rate without affecting the results derived. Only in Section 3.7 this is not the case.

(A4) *Employment*

Let N_t denote the number of persons capable of and wishing to work at time t and L_t the ones actually employed. When these numbers may change with rates n_t and l_t, respectively, for the employment ratio e_t it holds at time t

$$(3.6)\quad e_t = L_t/N_t = (1+l_t)L_{t-1}/(1+n_t)N_{t-1}, \quad t = 1,2,\ldots .$$

Unless otherwise stated we assume $e_t = 1$ or $L_t = N_t$, i.e. full employment of labor, and also full employment of the capital stock in each period $t = 1,2,\ldots$.

(A5) *Boundary Conditions*

In period $t = 0$, the economy starts with a positive capital stock $K_0 > 0$. For the case of a finite planning horizon $T > 1$ a positive final capital stock $K_T > 0$ is required.[1)]

---

1) If the control variables of the subsequent sections are assumed unrestricted, these assumptions suffice for the following analysis. In economic reality, however, we know that, e.g., the investment ratio, the wage rate, the saving ratios or even the employment rate, can not be chosen arbitrarily. If we wish to take account of such restrictions in our model economy, it is necessary to make much stronger and purely technical assumptions about the initial and final capital stock and, moreover, about the sequences of possible production functions and parameters. This would certainly hinder the understanding of the basic economics behind the models. Mathematically less elegant, but economically realistic, however, are the following requirements: First, both the initial and the final capital stocks are assumed to be sufficiently close to what in the next sections will be computed to be "optimal" capital stocks. Second, all the functions and parameters of the model may change only slightly between any two successive points of time.

next page ->

From these assumptions we deduce:

(D1) *Capital Development*

The capital stock in period t, K_t, is given by

$$K_t = a_t^w W_t + a_t^d D_t + u_t(F(K_{t-1}, L_{t-1}, t) - W_t - D_t) + (1-m_t)K_{t-1}, \quad t = 1,2,.. \tag{3.7}$$

or, equivalently,

$$K_t = (a_t^w - u_t)w_{t-1}L_{t-1} + (a_t^d - u_t)d_{t-1}L_{t-1} + u_t F(K_{t-1}, L_{t-1}, t) + (1-m_t)K_{t-1}, \quad t = 1,2,.. . \tag{3.8}$$

Thus, the investment ratio α_t, i.e. the ratio of gross investment to total GNP in period t, is given by

$$\alpha_t = u_t - \frac{(u_t-a_t^w)w_{t-1}L_{t-1} + (u_t-a_t^d)d_{t-1}L_{t-1}}{F(K_{t-1}, L_{t-1}, t)}, \quad t = 1,2,.. . \tag{3.9}$$

(D2) *Measurement of Workers' Share*

Usually, workers' share in output is measured by the wage ratio, i.e. the ratio of wages to the NNP, in period t given by

$$\beta_t = w_{t-1}L_{t-1}/(F(K_{t-1}, L_{t-1}, t) - m_tK_{t-1}). \tag{3.10}$$

-> In this context, note that in the dynamic models to be discussed, we call a sequence of states *feasible*, if there exists a corresponding sequence of controls taking on "realistic" values (in the sense of the requirements above) at any point of time.

Since in this work we mainly use the GNP rather than the NNP, we will define workers' share in period t by

$$(3.11)\quad \gamma_t = (w_{t-1} + d_{t-1})L_{t-1} / F(K_{t-1}, L_{t-1}, t)$$

in the model framework (A1) - (A5).

(D3) *Consumption*

We assume a closed economy or an open one in which imports equal exports in each period t. Since then total consumption C_t in the economy is the share of output which is not invested, we have

$$(3.12)\quad C_t = (1-\alpha_t)\, F(K_{t-1}, L_{t-1}, t), \qquad t = 1,2,\ldots .$$

By equations (3.8) and (3.9), we also see that C_t is a function $\tilde{C}_t: \mathbb{R}^2_+ \to \mathbb{R}_+$ of the capital stocks K_{t-1} and K_t if L_{t-1} and m_t are assumed fixed, i.e., in period $t = 1,2,\ldots$ we have

$$(3.13)\quad C_t = \tilde{C}_t(K_{t-1}, K_t) = F(K_{t-1}, L_{t-1}, t) + (1-m_t)K_{t-1} - K_t .$$

In each of the following seven sections, we work with the set of assumptions (A1) through (A5) and with a specific assumption (A6), in which the utility function to be maximized in the specific section is stated.

3.1 THE COOPERATIVE CASE

In economic reality investment and growth depend on a variety of decisions and objectives, e.g.,

- individual saving/consumption decisions from pursuing individual consumption objectives,
- individual or collective investment decisions related to various investment purposes,
- domestic and foreign decisions and actions influencing interest rates and capital flows,
- tax regulations stimulating or deterring investment or consumption,
- wealth distribution and the willingness to save and invest of different social groups in an economy.

It is certainly prohibitively difficult trying to make a "realistic" model taking account of all that and more. Therefore in the current and subsequent sections we make much simpler assumptions about the objectives governing people's decisions and actions. Here in this section it is assumed that all groups in the economy cooperate perfectly and have the ability to decide about the value of investment in each period according to their aggregate objectives.

In addition to the set of assumptions (A1) through (A5), for this section we state the following assumption:

(A6.1) *Utility from Consumption*

The model economy's society is able to attach a value V to each possible sequence of consumptions $\{C_t\}_{t=1,2,...}$. This states that for the case of a finite planning horizon T[1] there exists an aggregate utility function $U^c: \mathbb{R}^T \to \mathbb{R}$, i.e.,

$$V = U^c(C_1, C_2, .., C_T).$$

This utility function is assumed to be nondecreasing, continuously differentiable twice, and concave with respect to all arguments.

If the groups in the economy cooperate perfectly, it seems reasonable to assume that they want to maximize their utility from total consumptions rather than seeking to pursue any other individual objectives. By assumption (A6.1), the problem is to find the utility maximizing sequence of optimal investment ratios $\{\alpha_t^*\}_{t=1,2,..}$;[2] formally, for the finite planning horizon T, we have the problem to

$$\text{Maximize } U^c(C_1, C_2, .., C_T)\text{[3]}$$

(UP3.1) subject to

$$\left.\begin{aligned} C_t &= (1-\alpha_t)\ F(K_{t-1},\ L_{t-1},\ t) \\ K_t &= \alpha_t\ F(K_{t-1},\ L_{t-1},\ t)+(1-m_t)K_{t-1} \end{aligned}\right\}\ t=1,2,..$$

K_O, K_T specified .

1) In this work, the analysis will be restricted to this case of a finite planning horizon T. All the results of the subsequent sections, however, may be extended to the case where $T \to \infty$. This can be done similarly as shown in Buhl [1983].

2) Thus, in this section note the control variables are α_t, t=1,..,T.

3) Throughout this work, for both technical and economical reasons all maxima are assumed to exist.

Notice, here we have a classical problem of optimal economic growth which, based on the famous work of Ramsey [1928] and Solow [1956], in a continuous framework has been thoroughly analyzed in the last decades. Recently, discrete models mainly dealing with questions of existence, stability, and monotonicity have been analyzed by Benhabib/Nishimura [1984], Majumdar/Nermuth [1982], and Mitra/Ray [1984]. Although very interesting results have been obtained, we will not go into details now. Here problem (UP3.1) will be solved and discussed only briefly, because its only purpose in this chapter is to serve as a reference solution for the next sections' results.

Problem (UP3.1) is a special problem (UP) from Chapter 6, for which conditions (IA) from there are obviously satisfied. Thus, we may apply Theorem 6.1 to obtain:

3.1.1 Theorem

Let the assumptions (A1) through (A6.1) be satisfied for problem (UP3.1). If there exists a feasible sequence[1] of capital stocks $\{K_t^*\}_{t=0,1,2,..,T}$ satisfying the equation system

$$(3.1.2) \quad F_K(K_{t-1},L_{t-1},t) = \left[\frac{\partial U^c}{\partial C_{t-1}} \Big/ \frac{\partial U^c}{\partial C_t}\right]^{2)} + m_t - 1, \; t=2,..,T,$$

then it constitutes a sequence of optimal capital stocks for problem (UP3.1), and the sequence of optimal investment ratios

---

1) See footnote 1 on page 25.

2) By this abbreviation of the partial derivatives of the utility function, loosely referred to as marginal utility in period t, we mean

$\frac{\partial U^c}{\partial C_t}(C_1,..,C_T)\big|_{C_\tau = \tilde{C}_\tau(K_{\tau-1},K_\tau)}, \; \tau=1,..,T.$

Note, $K_0=K_0^*$ and $K_T=K_T^*$ need not satisfy the optimality conditions (3.1.2).

$\{\alpha_t^*\}_{t=1,..,T}$ is given by

$$(3.1.3)\quad \alpha_t^* = \frac{K_t^* - (1-m_t)\, K_{t-1}^*}{F(K_{t-1}^*, L_{t-1}, t)}, \quad t = 1,2,..T.$$

Notice, if marginal utility in period t is equal to the one in period t-1, from equation system (3.1.2) we obtain for $t = 2,..,T$

$$(3.1.4)\ F_K(K_{t-1}, L_{t-1}, t) = m_t .$$

Thus, each optimal capital stock is characterized by the marginal productivity being equal to the depreciation rate. For instance, this is the case if the utility function with respect to all arguments is linear with the same slope and thus there is no time preference. It is also true if simultaneously

(i) the utility function is symmetric with respect to all arguments and

(ii) labor, the production function, and the depreciation rate are constant in time, and

(iii) the initial capital stock is equal to the final one and satisfies equation (3.1.4).

3.1.5 Example

Let the utility function be given by

$$(3.1.6)\ U^c(C_1, C_2, .., C_T) = (C_1 \cdot C_2 \ .. \ C_T)^{1/2}$$

and the production functions by

$$(3.1.7)\ F(K_{t-1}, L_{t-1}, t) = cK_{t-1} + dL_{t-1}, \quad t = 1,2,.. ,$$

$m_t = c > 0$, $d \geqq 0$ and $L_t = L_0$ for all t.

Obviously, any initial capital stock K_0 satisfies equation (3.1.4). Now consider the sequence of capital stocks where $K_t = K_0$ for all $t = 1,..,T$. Of course, all K_t satisfy equation (3.1.4) and because of all consumptions $C_t = \tilde{C}_1(K_1,K_0)$, $t = 1,..,T$, marginal utilities are equal to each other and the equation system (3.1.2) is satisfied for all t. Thus, any sequence of time constant capital stocks is an optimal one.

3.1.8 Example

Now, let the utility function be

$$(3.1.9)\quad U^c(C_1,..,C_T) = C_1 \cdot C_2 \cdot\cdot \cdot C_T ,$$

and the production functions be

$$(3.1.10)\quad F(K_{t-1},L_{t-1},t) = cK_{t-1}^{1/2}\, L_{t-1}^{1/2} ,\ c>0,\ t=1,2,..$$

and again $m_t = m$ and $L_t = L_0$ for all t.

Obviously the initial capital stock satisfies equation (3.1.4) if

$$(3.1.11)\quad K_0 = L_0 c^2 / 4m^2 .$$

Again, consider the case when all $K_t = K_0$, $t = 1,..,T$, and consequently all capital stocks satisfy equation (3.1.4). Also, it is clear, that all period consumptions and thus marginal utilities are equal to each other implying that the capital stocks satisfy the equation system (3.1.2). Thus, the sequence of time constant capital stocks is optimal.

Notice, in the two preceding examples, the optimal capital stocks derived did not depend on the utility function specifically used. To see this, just interchange the utility functions

(3.1.6) and (3.1.9) and observe that the same (sequences of) capital stocks are optimal.

Frequently, the utility function $U^C: \mathbb{R}^T \to \mathbb{R}$ is assumed to be additively separable such, that there exist functions $U_t^C: \mathbb{R} \to \mathbb{R}$, $t = 1,2,..,T$, and

$$(3.1.12)\quad U^C(C_1,..,C_T) = \sum_{t=1}^{T} U_t^C(C_t) \prod_{j=0}^{t-1} (1+i_j)^{-1} ,$$

where $i_t \in [0,\infty)$[1] is the time preference rate from period t. In this case, by Corollary 6.2, we obtain from equations (3.1.2) the optimality conditions for the optimal capital stocks

$$(3.1.13)\quad F_K(K_{t-1},L_{t-1},t) = \frac{U_{t-1}^{C'}(\tilde{C}_{t-1}(K_{t-2},K_{t-1}))}{U_t^{C'}(\tilde{C}_t(K_{t-1},K_t))}(1+i_{t-1})+m_t-1, \qquad t = 2,..,T.$$

Note, if here in two subsequent periods marginal utilities are identical, we have

$$(3.1.14)\quad F_K(K_{t-1}, L_{t-1}, t) = i_{t-1} + m_t , \qquad t = 2,..,T.$$

As the following example shows, this observation can again be used to derive sequences of optimal capital stocks in special cases.

---

1) A negative time preference rate $i_t > -1$ would not alter the analysis.

3.1.15 Example

Assume the period utility functions U_t^c: $\mathbb{R} \to \mathbb{R}$, $t = 1,..,T$, are all equal to each other and the production functions are given by

$$(3.1.16)\quad F(K_{t-1},L_{t-1},t) = cK_{t-1}^{b}L_{t-1}^{1-b}\ ,\ b \in (0,1),\ t = 1,2,..\ ,$$

and $m_t = m$, $L_t = L$, $i_t = i$ for all t, where $i+m > 0$.

Then the time constant sequence of capital stocks, where

$$(3.1.17)\quad K_t = L\left[\frac{b \cdot c}{i + m}\right]^{1/(1-b)}, \qquad t = 0,..,T\ ,$$

satisfying equations (3.1.14) also satisfies the equation system (3.1.2) because of all consumptions being equal to each other. Thus the capital stocks are optimal and the optimal investment ratio, also constant in time, is given by

$$(3.1.18)\quad \alpha_t = \alpha = b \cdot m\ /\ (i + m)\ , \qquad t = 1,2,..,T.$$

Notice, for $i > 0$, i.e. the time preference being strictly positive, the optimal investment ratio is strictly smaller than b, the capital elasticity of output.

Specializing further, we may maximize the present value of consumption instead of utility from consumption. Due to the difficulties associated with questionable future utility functions, this approach was often analyzed in the theory of optimal economic growth. In other words, the utility function is now given by

$$(3.1.19)\quad U^c(C_1,..,C_T) = \sum_{t=1}^{T} C_t \prod_{j=0}^{t-1} (1+i_j)^{-1}\ .$$

It follows straight from Theorem 3.1.1, that any feasible sequence of capital stocks $\{K_t^*\}_{t=0,..,T}$ satisfying the equation system

(3.1.20) $F_K(K_{t-1}, L_{t-1}, t) = i_{t-1} + m_t$, $\quad t = 2,..,T$

constitutes a sequence of optimal capital stocks for problem (UP3.1), where the utility function is given by (3.1.19).

From equations (3.1.20) we learn that, due to the concavity of the production functions, for larger values of the time preference or depreciation rates the optimal capital stocks are smaller. By defining $k_t = K_t/L_t$ as the per capita capital stock and $f_t: \mathbb{R}_+ \to \mathbb{R}_+$ as the per capita production function in period t, i.e.,

(3.1.21) $f_t(k_{t-1}) = F(k_{t-1}, 1, t)$, $\quad t = 1,2,..,$

due to the linear homogeneity of the production function we obtain from equations (3.1.20)

(3.1.22) $f_t'(k_{t-1}) = i_{t-1} + m_t$, $\quad t = 2,..,T.$

Of course, if there exists a feasible sequence of capital stocks $\{K_t^*\}_{t=0,..,T}$ satisfying equations (3.1.20), by definition there also exists a sequence of optimal per capita capital stocks $\{k_t^*\}_{t=0,..,T}$ satisfying equations (3.1.22). These sequences are unique if, for all t = 2,..,T, $(f_t')^{-1}$, the inverse of the derivative, exists in a neighborhood of $i_{t-1} + m_t$. Economically, this condition means that each (per capita) production function is strictly concave in a neighborhood of the respective optimal (per capita) capital stock. Thus, in this case we have explicit solutions for the optimal capital stocks and investment ratios

$$(3.1.23)\quad k_t^* = (f'_{t+1})^{-1}(i_t + m_{t+1}) \,, \qquad t = 1,..,T-1\,,$$

$$(3.1.24)\quad K_t^* = L_t(f'_{t+1})^{-1}(i_t + m_{t+1}) \,, \qquad t = 1,..,T-1\,,$$

$$(3.1.25)\quad \alpha_t^* = \frac{(1+l_t)k_t^* - (1-m_t)k_{t-1}^*}{f_t(k_{t-1}^*)} \,, \qquad t = 1,..,T.$$

Finally, we investigate the case in which functions and parameters are constant in time, i.e., $f_t = f$, $i_t = i$, $m_t = m$, and $l_t = l$ for all t. Again we assume $i+m > 0$.

From equation (3.1.23) through (3.1.25) it follows:

3.1.26 Result

If the functions and parameters are constant in time, then so are both, the optimal per capita capital stock from period 1 through T-1 and the optimal investment ratio from period 2 through T-1. The optimal capital stock in each period increases with rate l, i.e. proportional to the increase of labor.

Defining the capital elasticity of output

$$(3.1.27)\quad \eta(k) = f'(k)\cdot k/f(k) \,,$$

the optimal investment ratio is given by

$$(3.1.28)\quad \alpha_t^* = \alpha^* = \eta(k^*)(l+m)/(i+m) \,, \qquad t = 2,..,T-1.$$

This result follows from multiplying the right-hand-side of equations (3.1.25) by $f'(k^*)/(i+m) = 1$ and using equation (3.1.27). Thus the optimal investment ratio is proportional to the capital elasticity of output.

After this step into the theory of economic growth some remarks on two important controversies seem appropriate now.

Finite versus infinite planning horizon

The emphasis in this work clearly lies on discrete time, finite horizon models. This constitutes a major difference to most of the other publications on the theory of economic growth. In fact, most authors worked with infinite horizons and considered their approach as the only justifiable one. Due to a number of problems arising from such an approach few researchers analyzed the implications of a finite planning horizon. Usually the purpose of these exercises was to obtain approximations for the infinite horizon case: E.g., see Hammond [1975], Mirrlees [1973], Phelps/Pollak [1968], and v.Weizsäcker [1967] . All these papers deal with "approximate optimal", "second best", "agreeable", or "fairly good" plans. Whenever the purpose of using a finite horizon was different from obtaining approximations, however, the papers sometimes caused quite controversial discussions: E.g., see Chakravarty [1962], [1966],Maneschi [1966a], [1966b].

With respect to these discussions it is interesting to note that for the models presented here the optimal saving, investment or wage policy may in fact be independent of a sufficiently large finite or infinite planning horizon. I have already mentioned on page 29 that the results may be extended to the case of an infinite planning horizon similarly as shown in Buhl [1983]. We will briefly sketch the proof-idea here: Suppose there exists an optimal policy for the infinite horizon case different from the one for some finite horizon T. Then there exists some period $\bar{T} < \infty$, such that the infinite horizon policy is better for all $t > \bar{T}$. Obviously, this is a contradiction to the result that for sufficiently large finite planning horizons, the finite horizon policies are all the same. Thus, even if it is impossible in a society to reach agreement on an adequate planning horizon, the optimal policies and states for all different, but sufficiently large, planning horizons is still exactly the same. Note that this reads "exactly the same"; these independence-results have nothing to do with the approximation approaches in the papers mentioned above. As these independence-results indicate, the discussion about finite versus infinite planning horizons proves rather fruitless for the kinds of problems to be presented in this chapter. But this did not justify to work with a finite horizon assumption from the beginning, i.e., before these independence-results are obtained.

The reason for doing so mainly stem from the author's uneases and doubts about the practical implications of technological progress, infinite horizon models, which were never discussed in the literature. By assuming exponential growth of population or technology these models usually imply for an optimal investment policy exponential growth of nearly everything, i.e., consumption, capital stock, GDP, and investment. We do not have to point to Meadows [1972] or Mesarovic/Pestel [1974] to show that exponential growth causes serious problems in relatively short-term finite horizons already. To suppose that exponential growth is feasible for an infinite horizon, however, seems much too gross an assumption as to be acceptable.

This example shows that often it is not sufficient merely to look at the assumptions of a model in order to check whether it may give guidance for practical applications. It is just as important, to check the consequences of obtained results against whatever was neglected in the assumptions. Many factors can be neglected for short-term considerations, but few for infinite planning horizons.

Another objection against using an infinite horizon is of similar nature: As economists we know how many difficulties we already have with short-term predictions. How much more difficult is it then, to forecast long-term future developments in the economy? It seems far fetched, again, and certainly to overstretch human imaginations having to make reasonable assumptions e.g. about the change of the production function for an infinite planning horizon. This is particularly important if today's irreversible decisions such as public investments for roads, rails e.t.c. crucially depend on these assumptions.

Of course, proponents of an infinite horizon will argue: All these arguments are technical obstacles and make it more difficult to follow ethical principles by using an infinite horizon. But why should it be better then to use a finite horizon, which is ethically indefensible if mankind is assumed to live forever? Considering today's arms race and the big risk of a nuclear holocaust, many people doubt for both probabilistic and human reasons if mankind is to live forever. There are even more who doubt whether the large capital stock for our posterity's benefit will at least partially be destroyed some day. Clearly, if this is possible to happen in the sense of a minimum constant probability in each period, we know that in the long run it will happen. And then *ex-post* it would turn out that our "care" for posterity was everything else but optimal for mankind. But even if such thoughts are much too pessimistic and mankind is to live without such problems forever, it still seems appropriate to analyze the implications of the finite horizon case, because such an approach respresents the way many people think the closest. And unless it is shown that such a short-term policy is worse than a long-term policy, the author believes it to be justifiable.

Discounting future consumption ?

Although we include the case of undiscounted future consumption, i.e. of no time preference, in our analysis, discounted future consumption is considered in our approach. Many authors on the theory of economic growth included discounting in their analysis, for instance Bose [1968], Goldman [1968], Hamada [1967], Infante/Stein [1973], Mirrlees [1967], Ryder/ Heal [1973], Stanley [1978], and others.

v.Böhm-Bawerk [1921] justified discounting:[1] ....."we feel less concerned about future sensations of joy and sorrow simply because they do lie in the future. Consequently we accord to goods which are intended to serve future ends a value which falls short of the true intensity of their future marginal utility." On the other hand Harrod [1948][1] called "pure time preference"....."a polite expression for rapacity and the conquest of reason by passion". He held that "time preference in this sense is a human infirmity, probably stronger in primitive than in civilized man".

It would be far beyond the scope of this section to reflect and discuss the controversy about discounting in the literature on economic growth. Thus we restrict ourselves to one more argument in favor of discounting, which, to our knowledge, appears nowhere else in the literature. Again, we point to the results implied by a discounting assumption rather than to rest our argument solely on the basic assumption. Economic models with positive discounting in the literature as well as the ones to be presented here imply less growth than their undiscounted counterparts (see, for instance, Sections 3.2 through 3.5). Usually, limits to growth such as scarce resources, pollution, e.t.c. are neglected in the assumptions. Since higher growth rates imply a higher need for resources and energy and more pollution, if the corresponding assumptions are not extremely favorable, the question arises: Is it really preferable to exhaust posterity's resources and environment in favor of a larger capital stock? Can we assume that posterity will meet the challenge and find the fuel to use it? Based on the results of a resource model in Buhl [1983], one may argue that a society should discount future consumption according to increasing efficiency in using the scarcest resource. Then sufficient resources may be left for an infinite horizon. Thus discounting future consumption in actual policy may yield a very conservatory and beneficial effect in favor of posterity's resources and environment.

---

[1] c.f. Koopmans [1967].

3.2 WHEN WORKERS CONTROL WAGES

Average wages paid in an economy depend on and influence directly or indirectly a lot of other economic factors. These are, for instance,

- the relative scarcity and education of the employees or workers,
- the quality, size, age, and value of the economy's capital stock,
- the bargaining power of the different groups in the society,
- the competitiveness of the economy in international trade,
- political and ethical values in the society.

As mentioned in Chapter 2 already, workers do have some limited control over wages. Therefore in this section we follow Lancaster's, Hoel's, Pohjola's and Machaczek's approaches and give the workers full control to set (average) wages. In other words, we investigate the question: How would, in the dynamic model framework (A1) through (A5), workers set wages if only they could control them and all other functions and parameters in the economy were exogeneously specified?

Suppose the existence of trade unions concentrating on wage income. It then seems reasonable to assume them to choose such a sequence of average wages $\{w_t\}_{t=0,..,T-1}$ or total wages $\{W_t\}_{t=1,..,T}$, which is best with respect to their objective. Thus, we substitute the following assumption (A6.2) for assumption (A6.1):

(A6.2) *Utility from Total Wages*

The group of workers is capable of attaching a value V to each possible sequence of total wages $\{W_t\}_{t=1,..,T}$. Thus, for the workers there exists an aggregate utility function $U^W: \mathbb{R} \to \mathbb{R}$, i.e.

(3.2.1) $V = U^W(W_1,..,W_T)$.

Just like other utility functions, $U^W\colon \mathbb{R}^T \to \mathbb{R}$ is assumed to be nondecreasing, continuously differentiable twice, and concave with respect to all arguments.

Now we can formulate the workers' problem, to

Maximize $U^W(W_1,..,W_T)$
subject to

$$\text{(UP3.2)}\quad \left.\begin{aligned} W_t &= w_{t-1}\, L_{t-1} \\ K_t &= u_t F(K_{t-1},L_{t-1},t)+(1-m_t)K_{t-1} \\ &\quad -(u_t-a_t^w)w_{t-1}L_{t-1}-(u_t-a_t^d)d_{t-1}L_{t-1} \end{aligned}\right\}\quad t = 1,..,T$$

K_0, K_T specified.

Notice, for $u_t \leq a_t^w$ the dynamic equation for K_t is non-decreasing with respect to w_{t-1}. Thus the workers may increase their wage rate and therefore their utility without decreasing the subsequent capital stock. Clearly in this case it would be optimal for them to set the average and total wages such that

$$\text{(3.2.2)}\quad W_t = F(K_{t-1},L_{t-1},t) - D_t\,, \qquad t = 1,..,T.$$

Thus, if the workers' propensity to save is at least as large as the capitalists' one, problem (UP3.2) is trivial. Workers would set wages such that nothing remains left for the capitalists.

For $u_t > a_t^w$, however, the situation is different. For larger values of the average wage rate w_t, the next periods' capital stock is smaller. Therefore future output to be distributed is also smaller and, depending on the workers' utility function, workers' total utility may be smaller for larger values of w_t, $t = 0,..,T-1$.

Obviously, the case $u_t > a_t^w$, $t = 1,..,T$, is the interesting one and will be investigated in the remainder of this section.

The following theorem can either be proved by solving the dynamic equation of K_t for w_{t-1}, plugging the result into the dynamic equation for W_t and deriving the optimality conditions for U^W as a function of $K_1,..,K_{T-1}$ or by applying Theorem 6.1.

3.2.3 Theorem

Let the assumptions (A1) through (A5) and (A6.2) be satisfied for problem (UP3.2) and $u_t > a_t^w$ for all $t = 1,..,T$. If there exists a feasible[1] sequence of capital stocks $\{K_t^*\}_{t=0,..,T}$ satisfying the equation system

$$(3.2.4)\quad F_K(K_{t-1},L_{t-1},t) = \frac{1}{u_t}\left[\frac{u_t-a_t^w}{u_{t-1}-a_{t-1}^w}\left[\frac{\partial U^W}{\partial W_{t-1}}\Bigg|\frac{\partial U^W}{\partial W_t}\right]+m_t-1\right]^{2)},$$

$$t = 2,..,T$$

then it constitutes a sequence of optimal capital stocks for problem (UP3.2), and the sequences of optimal average and total wages, $\{w_t^*\}_{t=0,..,T-1}$ and $\{W_t^*\}_{t=1,..,T}$ are given by

1) Recall that for feasiblity of a sequence of capital stocks or wage rates it is necessary that for all t we have $0 \leq W_t \leq F(K_{t-1},L_{t-1},t) - D_t$, $t = 1,..,T$.

2) Again, this abbreviation of the partial derivatives of the utility function stands for

$$\frac{\partial U^W}{\partial W_t}(W_1,..,W_T)\Bigg|_{W_\tau=\tilde{W}_\tau(K_{\tau-1},K_\tau)}\ ,\quad \tau = 1,..,T.$$

$$(3.2.5)\quad w_t^* = \frac{u_{t+1}F(K_t^*,L_t,t+1)+(1-m_{t+1})K_t^*-(u_{t+1}-a_{t+1}^d)d_tL_t-K_{t+1}^*}{(u_{t+1}-a_{t+1}^w)L_t}$$

$t = 0,..,T-1$

and

$$(3.2.6)\quad W_t^* = \frac{u_tF(K_{t-1}^*,L_{t-1},t)+(1-m_t)K_{t-1}^*-(u_t-a_t^d)d_{t-1}L_{t-1}-K_t^*}{(u_t-a_t^w)}$$

$t = 1,..,T.$

Notice, if both marginal utilities and the differences between the investment/saving rates are the same in consecutive periods t-1 and t, then the optimality conditions (3.2.4) reduce to

$$(3.2.7)\quad F_K(K_{t-1},L_{t-1},t) = m_t/u_t\ , \qquad t = 2,..,T.$$

3.2.8 Remarks

Comparing equations (3.2.7) and (3.1.4), the corresponding result from the preceding section, we observe:

(i) For $u_t = 1$ both equations are equivalent. Thus, if capitalists invest all their residual income, the same optimal capital stocks are obtained as in the preceding section, where utility from total consumption was maximized. It is interesting to note that in the classical model of economic growth capitalists were assumed to invest all their income while workers were assumed to consume only.

(ii) For $u_t \in (a_t^w, 1)$ marginal productivity of capital is larger and thus the value of the capital stock is strictly smaller than in the preceding section. Thus, in the more realistic case, where capitalists consume part of their residual income, workers' control over wages leads to smaller capital stocks.

(iii) Surprisingly enough, the workers' propensity to save does not affect marginal productivity of the optimal capital stocks. This result checks with the one from Hoel [1975, p. 44], who also derived, in a somewhat different model framework with functions and parameters constant in time, that the marginal productivity does not depend on the workers' saving rate.

If the utility function is separable such, that there exist functions $U_t^W: \mathbb{R} \to \mathbb{R}$, $t = 1,..,T$, and

$$(3.2.9)\quad U^W(W_1,..,W_T) = \sum_{t=1}^{T} U_t^W(W_t) \prod_{j=0}^{t-1} (1+i_j)^{-1},$$

we obtain from the optimality conditions (3.2.4)

$$(3.2.10)\quad F_K(K_{t-1},L_{t-1},t) = \frac{1}{u_t}\left[\frac{u_t - a_t^W}{u_{t-1} - a_{t-1}^W}\,\frac{U_{t-1}^{W'}(\tilde{W}_{t-1}(K_{t-2},K_{t-1}))}{U_t^{W'}(\tilde{W}_t(K_{t-1},K_t))}(1+i_{t-1}) + m_t - 1\right], \qquad t = 2,..,T.$$

If, again, both marginal utilities and the differences between the investment/saving rates are equal in consecutive periods t-1 and t, we obtain

$$(3.2.11)\quad F_k(K_{t-1},L_{t-1},t) = \frac{1}{u_t}\,[i_{t-1} + m_t], \qquad t = 2,..,T.$$

Comparing equations (3.2.11) and (3.1.14) the remarks 3.2.8 apply again. Obviously, the optimality conditions (3.2.11) are also obtained if we maximize the present value of total wages instead of utility, i.e.,

$$(3.2.12)\quad U^W(W_1,..,W_T) = \sum_{t=1}^{T} W_t \prod_{j=0}^{t-1} (1+i_j)^{-1}$$

and, as above, the differences between the investment/saving rates are the same in all periods t. The latter will be assumed in the remainder without further notice.

3.2.13 Example

Just as in Example 3.1.15, let the utility functions $U_t^W: \mathbb{R} \to \mathbb{R}$, $t = 1,..,T$, be identical, let the production functions be the Cobb-Douglas function (3.1.16), and $m_t = m$, $L_t = L_0$, $i_t = i > 0$, $u_t = u$, $a_t^d = a_t^w = a$ for all t.

Then the time-constant sequence of capital stocks with

$$(3.2.14)\quad K_t = L_0 \cdot \left[\frac{bcu}{i+m}\right]^{1/(1-a)}, \qquad t = 0,..,T,$$

satisfies the optimality conditions (3.2.11) and, because of all total wages being identical, also satisfies equations (3.2.10). Thus we have a sequence of optimal capital stocks which, for $u \in (a,1)$, are strictly smaller than the ones from Example 3.1.15. The corresponding controls, the optimal wages, are obtained from equations (3.2.5).

The corresponding investment ratio, also constant in time, is given by

$$(3.2.15)\quad \alpha_t = \alpha = b \cdot m \cdot u \,/\, (i+m)\,,^{1)} \qquad t = 1,..,T.$$

Notice, the investment ratio is proportional to the capitalists' investment rate u and, again, only for u = 1 checks with the optimal one from the preceding section. It is also independent of the workers' saving rate a.

1) Notice, because of $i > 0$ and $b, u \in (0,1]$ we have $0 < \alpha < 1$. Thus, the denominators in equation (3.2.16) differ from zero.

We now turn to measurement of workers' share in our Example 3.2.13. First, after some computation and rearrangement using equations (3.2.15), the wage ratio (3.10) is

$$(3.2.16)\quad \beta_t = \beta = \frac{u-\alpha}{(u-a)(1-\alpha)} - \frac{d}{\alpha^{b/(1-b)}(1-m\alpha)}, \quad t = 1,..,T.$$

In deduction (D2), it was mentioned already, that in this work, we prefer to use the ratio of workers' share to total output as the measurement of workers' share. This is computed to be

$$(3.2.17)\quad \gamma_t = \gamma = \frac{u}{u-a}\left[1-\frac{mb}{i+m}\right], \qquad t = 1,..,T.$$

By using equations (3.2.15), we obtain for workers' share

$$(3.2.18)\quad \gamma_t = \gamma = \frac{u-\alpha}{u-a}, \qquad t = 1,..,T.$$

Notice, if for the capitalists', workers', and total investment ratios it holds

$$(3.2.19)\quad a \leqq \alpha < u,$$

workers' share satisfies $0 < \gamma \leqq 1$. As empirical evidence suggests, assumption (3.2.19) is not restrictive.

After this example we return to conditions (3.2.11) and, again, give explicit formulas for the optimal capital stocks when they are unique. If we maximize the present value of total wages (3.2.12) it follows by linear homogeneity from optimality conditions (3.2.11) for the optimal per capita capital stocks

$$(3.2.20)\quad f_t'(k_{t-1}) = (i_{t-1} + m_t)/\,u_t\,, \qquad t = 2,..,T.$$

Thus, if there exists a feasible sequence $\{k_t^*\}_{t=0,..,T}$ satisfying equations (3.2.20) and if there exists, for all t, $(f_t')^{-1}$, the inverse of the derivative, in a neighborhood of $(i_{t-1} + m_t)/\,u_t$, we obtain explicit formulas for the optimal capital stocks, namely

$$(3.2.21)\quad k_t^* = (f_{t+1}')^{-1}((i_t + m_{t+1})/\,u_{t+1})\,, \qquad t = 1,..,T-1,$$

and

$$(3.2.22)\quad K_t^* = L_t(f_{t+1}')^{-1}((i_t + m_{t+1})/\,u_{t+1})\,, \qquad t = 1,..,T-1.$$

Comparing these with formulas (3.1.23) and (3.1.24), again we find for $u_t < 1$ that, compared to the cooperative case, the optimal capital stocks are strictly smaller if workers control wages.

At the end of this section, we analyze the case in which functions and parameters are constant in time, i.e., $f_t = f$, $i_t = i$, $m_t = m$, $u_t = u$, $l_t = l$, $a_t^w = a_t^d = a$, and $d_t = d$.

For this case, we obtain the same result as in the preceding section, namely:

If the functions and parameters are constant in time, then so are both, the optimal per capita capital stock from period 1 through T-1 and the optimal wage rate from period 1 through T-2. The optimal capital stock in each period increases with rate l, i.e. proportional to the increase of labor.

Also, the corresponding investment ratio is constant in time from period 2 through T-1.

Using the equation for the capital elasticity of output (3.1.27), the investment ratio is

$$(3.2.23)\quad \alpha_t = \alpha = \eta(k^*)u(l+m)/(i+m)\ , \qquad t = 2,..,T-1.$$

This result is obtained by multiplying the right-hand-side of equation (3.1.25) by $f'(k^*)/[(i+m)/u] = 1$. Thus, the investment ratio in this section is, again, proportional to the capital elasticity of output. For the workers' share in output, it follows by linear homogeneity for the case considered

$$(3.2.24)\quad \gamma_t = \gamma = \frac{u}{u-a}\left[1-\frac{(l+m)k^*}{f(k^*)}\right]\ , \qquad t = 2,..,T-1.$$

Because of $f'(k^*) = (i+m)/u$ this yields by (3.1.27)

$$(3.2.25)\quad \gamma_t = \gamma = \frac{1}{u-a}\left[u-\frac{\eta(k^*)u(l+m)}{i+m}\right]\ , \qquad t = 2,..,T-1.$$

Thus, obviously, the result (3.2.18) also holds here, i.e., $\gamma = (u-\alpha)/(u-a)$.

<u>3.2.26 Example</u>

Assume the plausible numerical values: Capital elasticity $\eta(k) = 0.3$ for all k, depreciation rate $m = 0.1$, time preference rate 0.05, and labor growth rate $l = 0.02$. Then equation (3.1.28) yields the <u>cooperative optimal investment ratio</u> $\alpha^* = 0.24$.

Now, if capitalists invest 75% of their residual income and workers invest 4% of their wages and dividends, <u>workers optimal share</u> in output is $\gamma^* = 0.8$ and the corresponding <u>investment ratio</u> is $\alpha = 0.18$.

3.2.27 Remark

As mentioned in condition (3.2.19) already, we have to require in this section that workers' saving/investment rate is not larger than the investment ratio. This requirement is necessary for economic feasibility because otherwise workers' share would exceed total output, thereby making capitalists residual income negative and thus ensuring that total investment does not exceed the value which is optimal for the workers. Empirical evidence suggests, this phenomenon will not occur for realistic parameter values. If unrealistic parameter values are to be excluded before hand, we have to require

$$\begin{aligned}(a_t^w\, w_{t-1} + a_t^d\, d_{t-1})\, f_t\left((f_t')^{-1}\left(\frac{i_{t-1}+m_t}{u_t}\right)\right) \\ \leq (1+l_t)(f_{t+1}')^{-1}\left(\frac{i_t+m_{t+1}}{u_{t+1}}\right) - (1-m_t)(f_t')^{-1}\left(\frac{i_{t-1}+m_t}{u_t}\right),\end{aligned} \tag{3.2.28}$$

$$t = 1,..,T.$$

Unfortunately, there does not seem to be a requirement taking care of this problem that is both, economically interpretable and mathematically elegant.

3.3 WHEN CAPITALISTS CONTROL INVESTMENT

In Section 3.2 the capitalists' investment rates u_t, $t = 1,..,T$, and thus investment behavior was assumed to be exogeneously specified and workers could control wages accordingly. Now, in contrast, we consider a somewhat opposite view: It is therefore assumed that due to all the economic factors mentioned in the preceding Section 3.2 wages are exogeneously given and capitalists have full control to decide about their investments accordingly.

Hence, in the dynamic model framework (A1) through (A5), here it is investigated which investment rates u_t, $t = 1,..,T$, are "optimal" for the capitalists if this is the only control variable in the model.

Since, by assumption (A2), capitalists receive the residual

(3.4) $R_t = F(K_{t-1}, L_{t-1}, t) - W_t - D_t$, $t = 1,2,..$

and may consume $(1-u_t)R_t$ in each period t it seems reasonable to assume that capitalists choose such a sequence of investment rates $\{u_t\}_{t=1,..,T}$ maximizing the value they attach to the consumable residual sequence $\{R_t^c\}_{t=1,..,T}$, where $R_t^c=(1-u_t)R_t$. Hence we substitute the following assumption for the previously used assumptions (A6.1) or (A6.2):

(A6.3) *Utility from Capitalists' Residual*

The group of capitalists is capable of giving a value V to each possible sequence of consumable residuals $\{R_t^c\}_{t=1,..,T}$.

Thus, for the capitalists there exists an aggregate utility function $U^R: \mathbb{R}^T \to \mathbb{R}$,

(3.3.1) $V = U^R(R_1^c,..,R_T^c)$.

Like all the other utility functions being worked with, $U^R: \mathbb{R}^T \to \mathbb{R}$ is assumed nondecreasing, continously differentiable twice, and concave with respect to all arguments.

Now the capitalists' problem can be formulated:

$$\text{Maximize } U^R(R_1^c,..,R_T^c)$$

subject to

$$\text{(UP3.3)}\quad \left.\begin{aligned} R_t^c &= (1-u_t)[F(K_{t-1},L_{t-1},t)-W_t-D_t] \\ K_t &= u_t[F(K_{t-1},L_{t-1},t)-W_t-D_t] \\ &\quad + a_t^w W_t + a_t^d D_t + (1-m_t)K_{t-1} \end{aligned}\right\} \quad t = 1,..,T.$$

$$K_O, K_T \text{ specified.}$$

Obviously, problem (UP3.3) is also a special problem (UP) from Chapter 6 with conditions (IA) satisfied and we thus apply Theorem 6.1 to obtain:

3.3.1 Theorem

Let assumptions (A1) through (A5) and (A6.3) hold for problem (UP3.3). If there exists a feasible sequence of capital stocks $\{K_t^*\}_{t=0,..,T}$ satisfying the equation system

$$\text{(3.3.2)}\quad F_K(K_{t-1},L_{t-1},t) = \left[\frac{\partial U^R}{\partial R_{t-1}^c} \middle| \frac{\partial U^R}{\partial R_t^c}\right]^{1)} + m_t - 1,\ t = 2,..,T,$$

then it constitutes a sequence of optimal capital stocks for problem (UP3.3), and the sequence of optimal capitalists' investment rates is given by $\{u_t^*\}_{t=1,..,T}$, where

$$\text{(3.3.3)}\quad u_t^* = \frac{K_t^* - (1-m_t)K_{t-1}^* - a_t^w W_t - a_t^d D_t}{F(K_{t-1}^*,L_{t-1},t)-W_t-D_t}, \qquad t = 1,..,T.$$

1) By this abbreviation of the marginal utilities, again we mean

$$\frac{\partial U^R}{\partial R_t^c}(R_1^c,..,R_T^c)\Bigg|_{R_\tau^c=(1-u_\tau)R_\tau},\ \tau=1,..,T\ .$$

Notice, for

$$(3.3.4)\quad \left[\frac{\partial U^R}{\partial R^c_{t-1}} \;\middle|\; \frac{\partial U^R}{\partial R^c_t}\right] = \left[\frac{\partial U^c}{\partial C_{t-1}} \;\middle|\; \frac{\partial U^c}{\partial C_t}\right], \qquad t = 2,..,T,$$

i.e., the ratios of marginal utilities from consumable residual and total consumption being identical, optimality conditions (3.1.2) check with (3.3.2). Thus, the same capital stocks are optimal for both, problem (UP3.1) and problem (UP3.3).

The case where equalities (3.3.4) hold, is quite interesting: In the preceding section it was shown, that, except under very restrictive conditions (see Remark (3.2.8)), workers' control over wages usually leads to smaller optimal capital stocks than in the cooperative case (Section 3.1). One thus might have expected, that the same holds if capitalists control investment without caring about social or cooperative objectives. Under conditions (3.3.4) however, this is not the case - the same optimal capital stocks are obtained as in the cooperative case. Although these conditions may seem restrictive, too, they may not be qualified as unrealistic. Some may argue, that the ratio of the capitalists' marginal utilities is larger than the one of the whole society's marginal utilities from total consumption in reality, because the capitalists' time preference is larger than the whole society's one. Others might find a lot of good reasons why the opposite may be true. Thus, depending on which ratio is larger, even larger capital stocks than in the cooperative case may be optimal for the capitalists.

This result, of course, is seeking for explanation. Let us start the discussion with giving an explanation for the special case

$$(3.3.5)\quad \left[\frac{\partial U^R}{\partial R^c_{t-1}} \;\Big|\; \frac{\partial U^R}{\partial R^c_t}\right] = \left[\frac{\partial U^c}{\partial C_{t-1}} \;\Big|\; \frac{\partial U^c}{\partial C_t}\right] = 1 \,, \qquad t = 2,..,T,$$

i.e., the ratios of marginal utilities are both equal to one. In this case, from the optimality conditions (3.1.2) and (3.3.2) we obtain

$$(3.3.6)\quad F_K(K_{t-1},\, L_{t-1},\, t) = m_t \,, \qquad t = 2,..,T.$$

That is to say, no matter whether capitalists control investment or a cooperative investment policy is pursued marginal productivity of capital must equal the depreciation rate. To understand why capitalists carry out the same investments as in the cooperative case notice that all model parameters except investment were assumed exogeneously specified. Thus, the capitalists cannot influence employment and, by the exogeneity of the wage rate, they cannot even influence the wage bill by means of their investment policy. Even if wages and employment are so high as to drive their profits to zero or below, by equations (3.3.6) capitalists still carry out all investments with marginal productivity at least as large as the depreciation rate. This policy is still the best capitalists can do in our model framework because they have no choice to pay the wage bill or not.

Now consider the case when

$$(3.3.7)\quad \left[\frac{\partial U^R}{\partial R^c_{t-1}} \;\Big|\; \frac{\partial U^R}{\partial R^c_t}\right] < \left[\frac{\partial U^c}{\partial C_{t-1}} \;\Big|\; \frac{\partial U^c}{\partial C_t}\right], \qquad t = 2,..,T,$$

i.e., the ratios of the capitalists' marginal utilities are smaller than the ones from total consumption. Assume the existence of feasible policies for optimality conditions (3.1.2) and (3.3.2). Then, when capitalists control investment, the optimal capital stocks are larger than in the cooperative case. One case where inequalities (3.3.7) are likely to hold is when the capitalists' time preference rate is smaller than the society's one. Another one is when the marginal utility of period t's consumable residual is very large. Such factors, apart from the exogeneous specification of the model parameters, can yield the larger optimal capital stocks when capitalists control investment.

If the utility function is separable such, that there exist functions $U_t^R: \mathbb{R} \rightarrow \mathbb{R}$, $t = 1,..,T$, and

$$(3.3.8) \quad U^R(R_1^c,..,R_T^c) = \sum_{t=1}^{T} U_t^R(R_t^c) \prod_{j=0}^{t-1} (1+i_j)^{-1} ,$$

optimality conditions (3.3.2) read

$$(3.3.9) \quad F_K(K_{t-1},L_{t-1},t) = \frac{U_{t-1}^{R'}(R_{t-1}^c)}{U_t^{R'}(R_t^c)}(1+i_{t-1})+m_t-1, \quad t = 2,..,T.$$

If, specializing further, we maximize the present value of capitalists' consumable residual instead of utility, i.e.,

$$(3.3.10) \quad U^R(R_1^c,..,R_T^c) = \sum_{t=1}^{T} R_t^c \prod_{j=0}^{t-1} (1+i_j)^{-1} ,$$

we obtain the optimality conditions

$$(3.3.11) \quad F_K(K_{t-1},L_{t-1},t) = i_{t-1}+ m_t , \qquad t = 2,..,T.$$

Notice that these optimality conditions check with conditions (3.1.20). Thus, if capitalists maximize the present value (3.3.10) the same capital stocks are optimal as in the case of the society cooperatively maximizing the present value of total consumption (3.1.19). The economic interpretation of this identity is the same as the one given for the case (3.3.5).

As derived in Section 3.1 already, by the linear homogeneity of the production function, optimality conditions (3.3.11) also hold for the marginal productivity of the per capita production function:

$$(3.3.12)\quad f_t'(k_{t-1}^*) = i_{t-1} + m_t \,, \qquad t = 2,..,T.$$

The sequences of optimal per capita capital stocks $\{k_t^*\}_{t=0,..,T}$ and investment rates $\{u_t^*\}_{t=1,..,T}$ are unique if, for all $t = 2,..,T$, $(f_t')^{-1}$, the inverse of the derivative, exists in a neighborhood of $i_{t-1} + m_t$. Then we obtain the explicit solutions

$$(3.3.13)\quad k_t^* = (f_{t+1}')^{-1}(i_t + m_{t+1}) \,, \qquad t = 1,..,T-1$$

and

$$(3.3.14)\quad u_t^* = \frac{(1+l_t)k_t^* - (1-m_t)k_{t-1}^* - a_t^w w_{t-1} - a_t^d d_{t-1}}{f(k_{t-1}^*) - w_{t-1} - d_{t-1}}, \quad t = 1,..,T.$$

We now utilize the concavity of the production functions and equations (3.3.13) and (3.3.14) to conduct a sensivity analysis:

<u>3.3.15 Remarks</u>

Ceteris paribus it holds:

(i) For larger values of the time preference rate i_t, the depreciation rate m_{t+1}, or both, the optimal per capita capital stock k_t^* must be smaller because the marginal productivity is larger.

By equations (3.3.14) the optimal investment rate u_t^* is also smaller in this case.

(ii) The optimal investment rate u_t^* is larger, however, for larger values of i_{t-1}, m_t, or both. Notice, in this case all the terms $(1-m_t)$, k^*_{t-1}, and $f_t(k^*_{t-1})$ are smaller.

(iii) For larger values of the workers' saving rates a^w_t and a^d_t the capitalists' optimal investment rate u^*_t is smaller. Since the optimal capital stocks do not depend on the workers' saving rates total investment is the same, implying that the adverse effects just have compensated.

(iv) For larger values of the labor change rate l_t the optimal capitalist investment rate u^*_t is larger, too. Its value has no impact on the optimal per capita capital stocks, as equations (3.3.13) indicate.

We conclude this section by investigating the case of functions and parameters constant in time, i.e., $f_t = f$, $i_t = i$, $m_t = m$, $l_t = l$, $a^w_t = a^d_t = a$, $w_t = w$, $d_t = d$, for all t. To simplify the following analysis, again we require $i+m > 0$.

From equations (3.3.13) and (3.3.14) then follows:

3.3.16 Result

If the functions and parameters are constant in time, then so are both, the optimal per capita capital stock from period 1 through T-1 and the optimal capitalist investment rate from period 2 through T-1. The latter is then given by

$$(3.3.17)\quad u^*_t = u^* = \frac{(l+m)k^*-a(w+d)}{f(k^*)-w-d}, \qquad t = 2,..,T-1.$$

3.3.18 Example

Consider the following parameter values, which are not unrealistic for the west-german economy:

Depreciation rate $m = 0.1$, labor change rate $l = 0$, workers' saving rate $a = 0.1$, capital-output ratio $k^*/f(k^*) = 3$, workers' share $\gamma = (w+d)/f(k^*) = 0.6$[1]. Then we obtain from formula (3.3.17) for the optimal capitalist investment rate $u^* = 0.6$. This value certainly does not stand in (sharp) contrast to empirical evidence and it would be interesting to investigate and compare the corresponding values in the industrialized world.

After this example we turn to investigation of distributional aspects. In our case considered where functions and parameters are constant in time and capitalists control investment the investment ratio is given by

$$(3.3.19) \quad \alpha_t = \alpha = \eta(k^*)(1+m)/(i+m) \;, \qquad t = 2,..,T-1.$$

For the workers' share in output, we obtain by linear homogeneity

$$(3.3.20) \quad \gamma_t = \gamma = \frac{1}{u-a}\left[1 - \eta(k^*)\frac{1+m}{i+m}\right] \;, \qquad t = 2,..,T-1.$$

Thus by utilizing the investment ratio α from formula (3.3.19), we obtain for the workers' and capitalists' shares, respectively

$$(3.3.21) \quad \gamma = (u-\alpha)/(u-a) \;, \qquad t = 2,..,T-1,$$

and

$$(3.3.22) \quad 1-\gamma = (\alpha-a)/(u-a) \;, \qquad t = 2,..,T-1.$$

---

1) To understand this parameter value, see deduction (D2) on page 26.

Notice again, that for the realistic requirement

$$(3.3.23) \quad a < \alpha < u ,$$

both shares satisfy $0 < \gamma , 1- \gamma < 1$. Economically, our theory makes sense only if condition (3.3.23) is satisfied. Mathematically, however, the analysis is valid also for the case of condition (3.3.23) being violated.

3.3.24 Example

Let the capital elasticity of output be given by $\eta(k^*)= 0.3$ and assume $l = i$. Then, by formula (3.3.19) the investment ratio is

$$(3.3.25) \quad \alpha = \eta(k^*) = 0.3 , \qquad t = 2,..,T-1.$$

Using the parameter values from Example (3.3.18), we obtain from equations (3.3.21) and (3.3.22) that the workers' and capitalists' shares are given by $\gamma = 0.6$ and $1- \gamma = 0.4$, respectively. Condition (3.3.23) is obviously satisfied for such and similar parameters.

3.4 THE NON-COOPERATIVE CASE OF WORKERS CONTROLLING WAGES AND CAPITALISTS CONTROLLING INVESTMENT

In Section 3.2 we determined optimal wage policies for the workers under the assumption that capitalists' investment behavior was given. Conversely in Section 3.3 we assumed wages (and other model parameters) exogeneously given and derived optimal investment policies for the capitalists accordingly.

Now it will be investigated under which conditions these two policies fit together in the following sense: When do there exist Nash equilibrium policies $(u^o,w^o):=\{u_t^o,w_t^o\}_{t\in\mathbb{N}}$ such that simultaneously

(i) Given capitalists' investment rates $u^o:=\{u_t^o\}_{t\in\mathbb{N}}$ workers' optimal wage policy is $w^o:=\{w_t^o\}_{t\in\mathbb{N}}$;

(ii) Given workers' wage rates w^o capitalists' optimal investment rates are u^o.

All the other model parameters and functions are, again, assumed exogeneously specified. Letting $J^w(u^o,w^o)$ and $J^c(u^o,w^o)$ denote workers' and capitalists' criteria, respectively, a Nash equilibrium satisfies as is well known

$$J^w(u^o,w^o) \geqq J^w(u^o,w) \text{ for all } w:=\{w_t\}_{t\in\mathbb{N}}$$

and

$$J^c(u^o,w^o) \geqq J^c(u,w^o) \text{ for all } u:=\{u_t\}_{t\in\mathbb{N}} .$$

Recall from deduction (D1) that the dynamic equation for the (sequence of) capital stocks is given by

$$\begin{aligned} K_t &= (a_t^w w_{t-1}+a_t^d d_{t-1})L_{t-1} + (1-m_t)K_{t-1} + \\ &\quad u_t(F(K_{t-1},L_{t-1},t) - (w_{t-1}+d_{t-1})L_{t-1}) , \qquad t=1,..,T. \end{aligned} \tag{3.4.1}$$

In the most general case considered, the optimality conditions for the sequence of capital stocks optimal for the workers are from Theorem 3.2.3

$$(3.4.2)\quad F_K(K_{t-1},L_{t-1},t) = \frac{1}{u_t}\left[\frac{u_t - a_t^w}{u_{t-1}-a_{t-1}^w}\left[\frac{\partial U^w}{\partial W_{t-1}}\bigg|\frac{\partial U^w}{\partial W_t}\right] + m_t - 1\right], t=2,..,T.$$

On the other hand the conditions for the optimal capital stocks of the capitalists were given in Theorem 3.3.1:

$$(3.4.3)\quad F_k(K_{t-1},L_{t-1},t) = \left[\frac{\partial U^R}{\partial R_{t-1}^c}\bigg|\frac{\partial U^R}{\partial R_t^c}\right] + m_t - 1 \quad , \quad t=2,..,T.$$

Now, obviously an equilibrium policy $\{u_t^o, w_t^o\}_{t\in\mathbb{N}}$ exists, if the following assumption is satisfied:

(A6.4) *Existence of a Dual Feasible, Optimal Policy*

There exists a sequence of feasible triples $\{K_t^o, u_t^o, w_t^o\}_{t\in\mathbb{N}}$ satisfying the dynamic equation (3.4.1) for all t with the property that optimality conditions (3.4.2) and (3.4.3) take on the same values for all t=2,..,T.

Notice that assumption (A6.4) is satisfiable only under quite restrictive conditions. For instance, the marginal productivities required in conditions (3.4.2) and (3.4.3) take on the same values only if the capitalists' investment rates are

$$(3.4.4)\quad u_t^o = \frac{a_t^w\left[\frac{\partial U^w}{\partial W_{t-1}}\bigg|\frac{\partial U^w}{\partial W_t}\right] + (1-m_t)(u_{t-1}^o - a_{t-1}^w)}{\left[\frac{\partial U^w}{\partial W_{t-1}}\bigg|\frac{\partial U^w}{\partial W_t}\right] + \left[1-m_t-\left[\frac{\partial U^R}{\partial R_{t-1}^c}\bigg|\frac{\partial U^R}{\partial R_t^c}\right]\right](u_{t-1}^o - a_{t-1}^w)}, t=2,..,T,$$

when the denominator is assumed different from zero.

Notice further that $u_t^o \leqq 1$ is not necessarily satisfied; this is true if and only if

$$(3.4.5)\quad \left[\frac{\partial \hat{U}^w}{\partial W_{t-1}}\middle|\frac{\partial U^w}{\partial W_t}\right](1-a_t^w) \gtreqless \left[\frac{\partial U^R}{\partial R_{t-1}^c}\middle|\frac{\partial U^R}{\partial R_t^c}\right](u_{t-1}^o - a_{t-1}^w),\ t=2,..,T.$$

If the two ratios of marginal utilities are equal to each other and workers' saving rates are the same, then conditions (3.4.5) are always satisfied.

In the remainder of this section we specialize our assumptions regarding both groups objectives and suppose they are maximizing the present values of wages and consumable residual, respectively. Thus the objective functions are given by (3.2.12) and (3.3.10). Moreover, we assume that the saving and investment rates are constant in time. The optimality conditions for the workers' and capitalists' optimal capital stocks are then given by

$$(3.4.6)\quad F_k(K_{t-1},L_{t-1},t) = f_t'(k_{t-1}) = \frac{1}{u}(i_{t-1} + m_t) \quad , \quad t=2,..,T$$

and

$$(3.4.7)\quad F_K(K_{t-1},L_{t-1},t) = f_t'(k_{t-1}) = i_{t-1} + m_t \quad , \quad t=2,..,T.$$

By comparing equations (3.4.6) and (3.4.7) we immediately see that sequences of (per capita) capital stocks simultaneously satisfying the optimality conditions for both, workers and capitalists exist only for $u=1$, i.e., capitalists invest all of their residual income. Then the optimality conditions coincide with the ones from the cooperative case considered in Section 3.1 .

Now suppose that for the cooperative case, where the present value of total consumption is maximized, there exist feasible sequences of capital stocks $\{k_t^*\}_{t=0,..,T}$ and $\{K_t^*\}_{t=0,..,T}$ satisfying the optimality conditions (3.4.7). Then assumption (A6.4) is satisfied for the sequence of triples $\{K_t^*,u_t^o,w_t^o\}_{t\in\mathbb{N}}$ and the Nash equilibrium policy is $\{u_t^o,w_t^o\}_{t\in\mathbb{N}}$, where

(3.4.8) $u_t^o = 1$, $t=0,..,T$

and

(3.4.9) $w_t^o = \dfrac{f_{t+1}(k_t^*)+(1-m_t)k_t^*-(1-a)d_t-(1+l_{t+1})k_{t+1}^*}{1-a}$, $t=0,..,T-1.$

We have thus derived

3.4.10 Result

Suppose capitalists and workers are maximizing the present values of consumable residual and wages, respectively. Let the saving and investment rates be constant in time. Then assumption (A6.4) is satisfiable if and only if there exist feasible capital stocks for the corresponding cooperative problem satisfying the optimality conditions and capitalists are "investing agents". Thus there exists a Nash equilibrium with capitalists investing all of their residual income. In this equilibrium, investments and capital stocks are optimal for the cooperative case, i.e., they maximize the present value of total consumption. The latter is solely enjoyed by the workers for capitalists consume nothing.

Specializing further, we now assume that the production function and all parameters are constant in time. It is clear from the preceding result that for the equilibrium policy derived the investment ratio is equal to the one from the cooperative case, i.e.,

(3.4.11) $\alpha_t = \alpha^* = \eta(k^*)(1+m)/(i+m)$, $t=2,..,T-1.$

Workers' share in output for u=1 is given by

(3.4.12) $\gamma_t = \gamma = \frac{1}{1-a}[1 - \eta(k^*)\frac{1+m}{i+m}]$, $t=2,..,T-1.$

Thus we have

$$(3.4.13) \quad \gamma_t = \gamma = (1-\alpha^*)/(1-a) \quad , \quad t=2,..,T-1.$$

From this expression we immediately see: If workers' saving rate a is equal to the optimal investment ratio α^* from the cooperative case, then workers' share in output γ is equal to 1, i.e., workers obtain total output. In this case they do not need the capitalists as investing agents. The other extreme is that workers' saving rate is zero. Then workers' share in output γ is equal to the consumption ratio $1 - \alpha^*$ from the cooperative case and capitalists' share $1 - \gamma$ is equal to the optimal investment ratio α^*. In other words, workers concede to the capitalists just that residual income which is necessary for optimal investment maximizing the present value of total consumption.

3.5 WHEN WORKERS CONTROL SAVING

While in Section 3.2 it was assumed that, apart from the other model parameters, workers'saving rates are exogeneously given and workers control the wage rate accordingly, now we consider another extreme. Thus, suppose that wages are determined by exogeneous factors such as competitiveness, bargaining power, traditional aspects, state regulations, collective contracts, and so on. Hence, in our model framework (A1) through (A5), workers can only influence the economy's investment behaviour via their own saving rates. Of course, we are aware of the fact that both extremes mentioned above simplify reality. In reality workers certainly have, within given boundaries, some limited control over wages and their saving rates as well. But analyzing both extremes definitely has two advantages: First, the impacts of the two control variables - wage rates and saving rates - upon the analysis are clearly isolated.

And second, it is certainly valuable to see the implications of extreme points, particularly if there is some indication that economic reality lies somewhere in between.

Workers' total income before saving is given by

(3.5.1) $B_t = W_t + D_t = (w_{t-1} + d_{t-1})L_{t-1}, \quad t = 1,..,T.$

Their consumption, i.e. the net income after saving/investment is

(3.5.2.) $N_t^W = [w_{t-1}(1-a_t^W) + d_t(1-a_t^d)]L_{t-1}, \quad t = 1,..,T.$

If workers have full control over their saving rates it seems reasonable that they choose these saving rates such as to maximize a criterion related to the sequence of incomes after saving/investment $\{N_t^W\}_{t\in\mathbb{N}}$. In this section we use the following assumption:

(A6.5) *Utility from Workers' Consumption*

The workers are able to give a value V to each possible sequence of consumptions, i.e. incomes after saving/investment $\{N_t^W\}_{t=1,..,T}$. Thus, again there exists an aggregate utility function $U^N: \mathbb{R}^T \to \mathbb{R}$, i.e.

$$(3.5.3)\ V = U^N(N_1^W,..,N_T^W).$$

Just like all the other utility functions applied here, $U^N: \mathbb{R}^T \to \mathbb{R}$ is assumed to be nondecreasing, continously differentiable twice, and concave with respect to all arguments.

Formally, the workers' problem investigated now is:

Maximize $U^N(N_1^W,..,N_T^W)$

subject to

$$\text{(UP.3.5)}\quad \left.\begin{aligned} N_t^W &= [w_{t-1}(1-a_t^W) + d_{t-1}(1-a_t^d)]L_{t-1} \\ K_t &= u_t F(K_{t-1},L_{t-1},t) + (1-m_t)K_{t-1} \\ &\quad -(u_t-a_t^W)w_{t-1}L_{t-1}-(u_t-a_t^d)d_{t-1}L_{t-1} \end{aligned}\right\}\ t=1,..,T.$$

K_o, K_T specified.

Recall that we have distinguished between the worker saving rate from wage income a_t^W and the one from dividend income a_t^d. This was done because of the empirical observation that the percentage of saving from wage income considerable differs from the percentage of saving from dividend income. In the current section, however, we are interested in determining workers'optimal amount of saving and the resulting optimal capital stocks. Hence it does not really matter from which source total saving comes. We could therefore use either a_t^W or a_t^d as the control variable or, equivalently, consider an average by assuming $a_t = a_t^W = a_t^d$. For the next result, it does not matter which approach is chosen because all of them lead to the same optimality conditions. In either case conditions (IA) from Chapter 6 are satisfied and we may therefore apply Theorem 6.1 to obtain:

3.5.4. THEOREM

Let assumptions (A1) through (A5) and (A6.5) be satisfied for problem (UP3.5). If there exists a feasible [1] sequence of capital stocks $\{K_t^*\}_{t=0,..,T}$ satisfying equations

$$(3.5.5)\quad F_K(K_{t-1},L_{t-1},t) = \frac{1}{u_t}\left[\left(\frac{\partial U^N}{\partial N_{t-1}^w} / \frac{\partial U^N}{\partial N_t^w}\right)^{1)} + m_t - 1\right],\ t=2,..,T,$$

then it constitutes a sequence of optimal capital stocks for problem (UP3.5). All sequences of saving rates $\{a_t^{w*}\}_{t=1,..,T}$ and $\{a_t^{d*}\}_{t=1,...,T}$ satisfying the dynamic equation for $\{K_t^*\}_{t=0,..,T}$, i.e.

$$(3.5.6)\quad K_t^* = u_t F(K_{t-1}^*,L_{t-1},t) + (1-m_t)K_{t-1}^*$$
$$- (u_t - a_t^w)w_{t-1}L_{t-1} - (u_t - a_t^d)d_{t-1}L_{t-1},\ t=1,..,T$$

are optimal saving rates for the workers.

Notice, if capitalists are investing agents with investment rate $u_t = 1$ and the ratios of marginal utilities are equal to the ones from Theorem 3.1.1, we obtain the same optimality conditions derived there. That is to say, the same capital stocks are optimal here as in the case of the society cooperatively maximizing their utiliy from total consumption.

We have mentioned in Section 3.3 already, that in the case of identical ratios of marginal utilities the same capital stocks are optimal for the capitalists and the cooperative society. Thus, from the above it is no surprise that if, moreover,

[1] See footnotes on page 25 and page 30.

capitalists are investing agents only, the same capital stocks are optimal for workers, capitalists, and the cooperative society.

It is also interesting to observe that for $u_t - a_t^w$ = const, t=1,..,T and the ratios of marginal utilities being identical, optimality conditions (3.5.5) check with the ones from Theorem 3.2.3. Hence, no matter whether workers control wages or their saving rates, the same capital stocks are, ceteris paribus, optimal for them.

As in the preceding sections we will now specialize the utility function. First, suppose it is separable such, that there exist functions $U_t^N: \mathbb{R} \to \mathbb{R}$, t=1,..,T, and

$$(3.5.7)\quad U^N(N_1^w,..,N_T^w) = \sum_{t=1}^{T} U_t^N(N_t^w) \prod_{j=1}^{t-1} (1+i_j)^{-1}.$$

Then we obtain from optimality conditions (3.5.5)

$$(3.5.8)\quad F_K(K_{t-1},L_{t-1},t) = \frac{1}{u_t}\left[\frac{U_{t-1}^{N'}(N_{t-1}^w)}{U_t^{N'}(N_t^w)}(1+i_{t-1}) + m_t - 1\right],\ t=2,..,$$

and may compare these with the corresponding results (3.1.13), (3.2.10), and (3.3.9). This leads to similar results as outlined above.

Second, we may assume that the workers wish to maximize the present value of their net incomes after saving, i.e., the utility function is given by

$$(3.5.9)\quad U^N(N_1^w,..,N_T^w) = \sum_{t=1}^{T} N_t^w \prod_{j=0}^{t-1} (1+i_j)^{-1}.$$

Then the optimality conditions are further simplified.

(3.5.10) $F_k(K_{t-1},L_{t-1},t) = (i_{t-1}+m_t)/u_t, \ t=2,..,T.$

Due to the problems associated with estimating intertemporal utility functions objectives like (3.5.9), where no utility function in the usual sense is needed, are certainly particularly important. We therefore compare all the corresponding results in the following

3.5.11 REMARKS *Maximizing the Present Values*

(i) Only if $u_t = 1$ for all t, the optimality conditions above (3.5.10) are equivalent to (3.1.20). Thus, if capitalists are investing agents only, then the same capital stocks are optimal for both, workers controlling their saving rates and the cooperative society controlling their investment ratio.

(ii) Only if $u_t - a_t^w$ = const for all t, optimality conditions (3.5.10) check with (3.2.11). Thus, if the difference between the capitalists'investment rate and workers' (wage) saving rate is constant in time, then the same capital stocks are optimal for the workers no matter whether they control wages or saving.

(iii) Only if $u_t = 1$ for all t, optimality conditions (3.5.10) are also indentical to (3.3.11).Thus, if the other model parameters are such that capitalists'optimal policy is to be investing agents only, then the same capital stocks are optimal for both, workers controlling saving and capitalists controlling investment.

(iv) Combining remarks (i) through (iii) we find:
Only for $u_t = 1$ and $a^w_t = a^w$ for all t, all optimality conditions (3.1.20), (3.2.11), (3.3.11), and (3.5.10) are equivalent. That is to say, if all model parameters and functions are such that

(iv.i) capitalists' optimal policy is to be investing agents only, and

(iv.ii) workers' optimal saving policy is a (wage) saving rate constant in time,

then the same capital stocks are optimal for the co-operative society, workers controlling wages or saving, and capitalists controlling investment. Notice that the conditions for which this holds are quite restrictive.

As was mentioned in the preceding sections already, all optimality conditions for the optimal capital stocks also hold for (the marginal productivity of) the optimal per capita capital stocks due to linear homogeneity. Here, the capital stocks are unique if there exists, for all t, $(f'_t)^{-1}$, the inverse of the per capita production function's derivative, in a neighborhood of $(i_{t-1}+m_t)/u_t$. The optimal per capita capital stocks are then given by

(3.5.12) $k^*_t = (f'_{t+1})^{-1}((i_t+m_{t+1})/u_{t+1})$, $t=1,..,T-1$.

For the rest of this section, just as previously, we turn to the case of functions and parameters constant in time, i.e., $f_t=f$, $i_t=i$, $m_t=m$, $u_t=u$, $l_t=l$, $w_t=w$, and $d_t=d$.

Since the optimality conditions and the optimal capital stocks themselves then are the same as in the case where workers control wages, the following results should not surprise:

(i) The optimal per capita capital stock is constant in time from period 1 through T-1.

(ii) The same holds for the optimal saving rate $a_t = a_t^w = a_t^d$ from period 2 through T-1, as inspection of the following form of the dynamic equation clearly indicates

$$(3.5.13)\quad a_t^* = \frac{(1+l)k_t^* - (1-m)k_{t-1}^* - u(f(k_{t-1}^*) - w - d)}{w + d}, \quad t=1,..,T.$$

If a_t^w is considered the control variable and the saving rate on dividend income $a_t^d = a^d$ assumed to be exogeneous or vice versa, then the optimal value of the respective control variable is also constant in time from period 2 through T-1. To see that consider

$$(3.5.14)\quad a_t^{w*} = \frac{(1+l)k_t^* - a^d d - (1-m)k_{t-1}^* - u(f(k_{t-1}^*) - w - d)}{w}, \quad t=1,..,T.$$

and

$$(3.5.15)\quad a_t^{d*} = \frac{(1+l)k_t^* - a^w w - (1-m)k_{t-1}^* - u(f(k_{t-1}^*) - w - d)}{d}; \quad t=1,..,T.$$

(iii) The corresponding investment ratio, also constant in time from period 2 through T-1, is given by

$$(3.5.16)\quad \alpha = \eta(k^*)u(l+m)/(i+m), \qquad t=2,..,T.$$

and checks with formula (3.2.23).

(iv) Worker's share in output is also constant in time from period 2 through T-1, namely

$$(3.5.17)\quad \gamma = \frac{1}{u-a}\left[u - \frac{\eta(k^*)u(1+m)}{i+m}\right], \qquad t=2,..,T-1,$$

or, equivalently,

$$(3.5.18)\quad \gamma = (u-\alpha)/(u-a), \qquad t=2,..,T-1,$$

where α and a are given by formulas (3.5.16) and (3.5.13), respectively.

3.5.19 EXAMPLE

Let the per capita production function be given by

$$(3.5.20)\quad f_t(k_{t-1}) = k_{t-1}^b,\ 0<b<1, \qquad t=1,..,T$$

and assume the plausible numerical values: Capital elasticity b=0.3, depreciation rate m=0.1, time preference rate i=0.02, capitalists' investment rate u=0.8, and labor growth rate l=0.02.

Since the time constant optimal per capita capital stock is given by

$$(3.5.21)\quad k^* = [bu/(i+m)]^{1/(1-b)}$$

and the corresponding per capita output is

$$(3.5.26)\quad f(k^*) = [bu/(i+m)]^{b/(1-b)},$$

we obtain by inserting the values above:

$$(3.5.27)\quad k^* = 2^{1/0\ 7} \sim 2.7$$

and

$$(3.5.28)\quad f(k^*) = 2^{0.3/0.7} \sim 1.35,$$

i.e., the capital output ratio is roughly equal to 2.

Now let wages and workers' dividends be given by w+d = 1 per capita. Then from equation (3.5.13) we obtain workers' optimal saving rate $a_t^* = 0.044$, i.e. workers save 4.4% of their total income. By equation (3.5.16) the corresponding investment ratio is given by $\alpha = 0.24$ and, by formula (3.5.18), workers'share is given by $\gamma \sim 0.74$.
It is interesting to compare these results with the ones obtained for the cooperative case by inserting the numerical values above.

The optimal per capita capital stock is there given by

$$(3.5.29)\quad k^* = [b/(i+m)]^{1/(1-b)} \sim 3.7,$$

the corresponding per capita output is

$$(3.5.30)\quad f(k^*) = [b/(i+m)]^{b/(1-b)} \sim 1.48,$$

i.e., the capital output ratio roughly equals 2.5. The optimal investment ratio is given by equation (3.1.28) and thus we obtain $\alpha^* = 0.3$.

If in this case capitalists are to invest 80% of their residual income and workers save and invest 4.4% of their total income then the following distribution is necessary: Workers' share is given by $\gamma = 0.6614$ and capitalists' share is $1-\gamma = 0.3386$. Thus, workers per capita income is given by $\gamma f(k^*) = 0.9789 < 1$, which is smaller than before, where w+d = 1.

3.6 THE NONCOOPERATIVE CASE OF CAPITALISTS CONTROLLING INVESTMENT AND WORKERS CONTROLLING SAVING

When deriving optimal investment policies for the capitalists in Section 3.3 it was assumed that workers' saving behavior and all the other model parameters were exogeneously given. On the other hand in Section 3.5, we determined optimal saving policies for the workers under the assumption that capitalists' investment behavior is given.

Here, similarly to Section 3.4, it will be investigated under which conditions these two optimal policies fit together in the following sense: When do there exist Nash equilibrium policies $\{u_t^o, a_t^o\}_{t\in\mathbb{N}}$[1] such that simultaneously

(i) Given workers' saving behavior $a^o := \{a_t^o\}_{t\in\mathbb{N}}$, capitalists' optimal investment policy is $u^o := \{u_t^o\}_{t\in\mathbb{N}}$;

(ii) Given capitalists' investment behavior u^o, workers' optimal saving policy is a^o.

Notice that both the workers' and the capitalists' criteria (3.5.3) and (3.3.1) are functions of $a := \{a_t\}_{t\in\mathbb{N}}$ and $u := \{u_t\}_{t\in\mathbb{N}}$. Thus $J^w(a,u)$ denotes the workers' criterion (3.5.3) and $J^c(a,u)$ denotes the capitalists' criterion (3.3.1).

Formally stated, the sequence of policies $\{u^o, a^o\}$ is a Nash equilibrium, if and only if

$$J^w(a^o,u^o) = J^w(a,u^o) \qquad \text{for all } a,$$

(3.6.1)

$$J^c(a^o,u^o) = J^c(a^o,u) \qquad \text{for all } u .$$

As is well known and obvious from the definition above, such a Nash equilibrium is dual stable in the following sense:

---

1) As was explained in the preceding section it is assumed here for simplicity of illustration only, that $a_t^w = a_t^d = a_t$ for all t.

If one group insists on choosing its equilibrium policy, then the other group cannot gain by choosing a strategy different from its equilibrium policy. Because of this dual stability, Nash equilibrium policies play an important role in non-cooperative game type situations. Just as previously, all the other model parameters and functions here and in the remainder are assumed exogeneous.

Recall that the dynamic equation for a sequence of capital stocks may be written as

$$(3.6.2)\quad K_t = u_t(F(K_{t-1},L_{t-1},t)-W_t-D_t)+a_t(W_t+D_t)+(1-m_t)K_{t-1}\ , \quad t=1,..,T.$$

In the most general case considered, the optimality conditions for the sequence of capital stocks optimal for the capitalists are from Theorem 3.3.1

$$(3.6.3)\quad F_K(K_{t-1},L_{t-1},t) = \left[\frac{\partial U^R}{\partial R^c_{t-1}} \bigg/ \frac{\partial U^R}{\partial R^c_t}\right] + m_t - 1 \quad , \quad t=2,..,T.$$

On the other hand the conditions for the optimal capital stocks of the workers according to Theorem 3.5.4 are

$$(3.6.4)\quad F_K(K_{t-1},L_{t-1},t) = \frac{1}{u_t}\left[\left[\frac{\partial U^N}{\partial N^w_{t-1}} \bigg/ \frac{\partial U^N}{\partial N^w_t}\right] + m_t - 1\right], \quad t=2,..,T.$$

Notice that both in Theorems 3.3.1 and 3.5.4 we had to require the existence of feasible capital stocks satisfying the dynamic equation (3.6.2) and the corresponding optimality condition (3.6.3) or (3.6.4). If such feasible capital stocks do not exist, there may still exist optimal policies for both groups constituting a Nash equilibrium solution. This is shown in the following example.

3.6.5 Example

Let the production function be given by

$$(3.6.6)\quad F(K_{t-1},L_{t-1},t) = K_{t-1} \quad , \qquad t=1,..,T,$$

and $K_o = 1$. Thus total output in period 1 is equal to 1. Now let the saving and investment rates be restricted to $a_t, u_t \in [0,0.6]$ for all t. Then gross investment in period 1 may not exceed 0.6. If $m_t = 0.1$ depreciation in period 1 is 0.1. Thus net investment may not exceed 0.5 in period 1, and by the same reasoning may not exceed 0.75 in period 2. Suppose T=2 and $K_2 = 9/4$. This final capital stock is attainable only for $a_1=a_2=u_1=u_2=0.6$. Therefore $\{u_t^o,a_t^o\}_{t=1,2}$, where $u_t^o=a_t^o=0.6$, t=1,2 , constitutes a Nash equilibrium policy but neither of the optimality conditions (3.6.3) or (3.6.4) may be satisfiable for the optimal capital stock $K_1^* = 1.5$.

For instance, if the utility functions $U^R: \mathbb{R}^2 \rightarrow \mathbb{R}$ and $U^N: \mathbb{R}^2 \rightarrow \mathbb{R}$ with respect to both arguments are linear with the same slope, then optimality condition (3.6.3) requires a marginal productivity of 1/10, whereas (3.6.4) requires a marginal productivity of 1/6 . The marginal productivity of the only feasible and thus optimal capital stock $K_1^* = 1.5$, however, is, as for K_o and K_2, $1 > 1/6 > 1/10$.

We learn from Example (3.6.5) that in case of nonexistence of feasible capital stocks satisfying the optimality conditions, these conditions do not help in our search for Nash equilibria. Thus we assume in the remainder.

(A6.6) *Existence of a Dual Feasible, Optimal Policy*
There exists a sequence of feasible triples $\{K_t^o,a_t^o,u_t^o\}_{t\in\mathbb{N}}$ satisfying the dynamic equation (3.6.2) for all t with the property that optimality conditions (3.6.3) and (3.6.4) take on the same values for all t=2,..,T.

It is obvious that under assumption (A6.6) the policy $\{a_t^o, u_t^o\}_{t \in \mathbb{N}}$ constitutes a Nash equilibrium satisfying conditions (3.6.1). Assumption (A6.6), however, is satisfiable only under quite restrictive conditions. For instance, the marginal productivitities required in the optimality conditions take on the same values only if the capitalists' investment rates are given by

$$(3.6.7)\quad u_t^o = \frac{\left[\dfrac{\partial U^N}{\partial N_{t-1}^w} \middle| \dfrac{\partial U^N}{\partial N_t^w}\right] + m_t - 1}{\left[\dfrac{\partial U^R}{\partial R_{t-1}^c} \middle| \dfrac{\partial U^R}{\partial R_t^c}\right] + m_t - 1}, \qquad t=2,..,T,$$

assuming the denominator is different from zero.

If the two ratios of marginal utilities are equal to each other, then (3.6.7) reads $u_t^o = 1$ for all t. Then assumption (A6.6) is satisfiable only if the capitalists are investing all of their residual income. Notice that the two ratios of marginal utilities are identical if capitalists and workers are maximizing the present values of their consumptions. In this case optimality conditions (3.6.3) and, for $u_t=1$, (3.6.4) check with the optimality conditions (3.1.20) from the cooperative case. We have thus derived:

3.6.8 Result

Suppose workers and capitalists are maximizing the present values of their respective consumptions. Then assumption (A6.6), guaranteeing existence of a Nash equilibrium, is satisfiable only if capitalists are investing agents investing all of their residual income.
If assumption (A6.6) holds, then the equilibrium policy is given by $\{u_t^o, a_t^o\}_{t \in \mathbb{N}}$, where $u_t^o = 1$ and

$$(3.6.9)\quad a_t^o = \frac{K_t^o - (1-m_t)K_{t-1}^o - u_t(F(K_{t-1}, L_{t-1}, t) - W_t - D_t)}{W_t + D_t}, \quad t=1,..,T.$$

The sequences of optimal equilibrium capital stocks $\{K_t^o\}_{t\in\mathbb{N}}$ and $\{k_t^o\}_{t\in\mathbb{N}}$ satisfy

$$(3.6.10)\quad F_k(K_{t-1}^o, L_{t-1}, t) = f'(k_{t-1}^o) = i_{t-1} + m_t \quad , \quad t=2,..,T.$$

That is to say, investments and capital stocks are optimal for the cooperative case, i.e., they maximize the present value of total consumption. Since capitalists are investing agents only, workers alone enjoy maximal total consumption.

3.7 THE NON-COOPERATIVE CASE OF CAPITALISTS CONTROLLING EMPLOYMENT AND WORKERS CONTROLLING WAGES

In all of the models discussed so far, total labor input L_t, t=0,..,T, was assumed to be exogeneously specified. If we consider free market economies with the two conflicting groups capitalists and workers, this assumption is certainly questionable. It is particularly questionable if we give workers full control over wages, but concede to the capitalists variation of investment only. In reality, capitalists would definitly choose employment depending on the wage rate controlled by workers.

Therefore in this section we suppose that in each period t capitalists may choose a labor input L_t that may depend on the wage rate, their objective, and the production situation but is independent of previous and future labor inputs $L_o,..,L_{t-1}$ and $L_{t+1},..,L_T$. Similar to Section 3.3 we assume here, according to assumption (A6.3), that capitalists wish to maximize utility from their (sequence of) consumable residual income, i.e.,

(3.7.1) Maximize $U^R(R_1^c,..,R_T^c)$,

where

(3.7.2) $R_t^c = (1-u_t)[F(K_{t-1},L_{t-1},t)-w_{t-1}L_{t-1}-D_t]$,[1] t=1,..,T.

The following theorem answers the question, what amount of labor input results from the capitalists objective:

---

[1] Workers' dividend income D_t, t=1,..,T, is assumed independent of labor input L_t, t=0,..,T. That is to say, contrary to the preceding sections we will not work with $d_t = D_{t+1}/L_t$ here.

<u>3.7.3 THEOREM</u>

Let the assumptions (A1) through (A5) and (A6.3) be satisfied and suppose for the capitalists' and workers' investment rates $u_t \in [0,1)$ and $u_t \geqq a_t^w$ for all t. If capitalists have full control over labor input L_t in each period independently, then for all t their optimal labor inputs L_t^*, if they exist, satisfy

$$(3.7.4)\quad F_L(K_{t-1}, L_{t-1}^*, t) = w_{t-1},\ t=0,..,T-1.$$

That is to say, marginal productivity of labor is equal to the wage rate.

Suppose for all t, $(F_L)^{-1}$, the inverse of the production functions partial derivative with respect to labor exists in a neighborhood of w_{t-1} and N_{t-1} is sufficiently large, then unique existence of the labor inputs $L_0^*,..,L_{T-1}^*$ is guaranteed.

<u>Proof</u>

Notice that equations (3.7.4) are first order conditions for optimality of the capitalists' consumable residuals (3.7.2) with respect to labor. The second order conditions are obviously satisfied due to $u_t<1$ and the production function's concavity for all t. Thus, if they exist, labor inputs $L_0^*,..,L_{T-1}^*$ maximize $R_1^C,..,R_T^C$. By the same argument, the labor inputs $L_0^*,..,L_{T-1}^*$ also maximize capitalists' <u>invested</u> residuals given by

$$(3.7.5)\quad R_t^I = R_t - R_t^C = u_t[F(K_{t-1}, L_{t-1}, t) - w_{t-1}L_{t-1} - D_t],\ t=1,..,T.$$

Therefore each labor input L_{t-1}^*, t=1,..,T is optimal for the capitalists with respect to both, consumption and investment in period t. Because of $u_t \geqq a_t^w$ a labor input $\hat{L}_{t-1} > L_{t-1}^*$ would not increase total investment in period t and thus K_t.

Due to the monotonicity of the production function each R_t^c is nondecreasing in K_{t-1}.

Since the utility function $U^R: \mathbb{R}^T \to \mathbb{R}$ is nondecreasing with respect to all $R_1^c,..,R_T^c$ obviously the labor inputs $L_o^*,..,L_{T-1}^*$ also maximize the utility function.

The second assertion of the Theorem is trivially seen by noting that the existence of $(F_L)^{-1}$ implies:

(i) strict concavity of each period's production function with respect to labor in a neighborhood of L_{t-1}^*,

(ii) $F_L(K_{t-1},L_{t-1},t) < w_{t-1} \;\forall\; L_{t-1} > L_{t-1}^*$,

(iii) $F_L(K_{t-1},L_{t-1},t) > w_{t-1} \;\forall\; L_{t-1} < L_{t-1}^*$.

Thus, unique existence is guaranteed for N_{t-1} sufficiently large. □

To sum up a few explanations to Theorem 3.7.3 and implications thereof, we state the following:

3.7.6 REMARKS

- An optimal labor input L_t^* does not exist if and only if either

  (i) $F_L(K_t,L_t,t+1) < w_t$ for $L_t \to 0$

  or

  (ii) $F_L(K_t,L_t,t+1) > w_t$ for all $0 < L_t \leqq N_t$

- Unique existence of an optimal labor input L_t^* is a priori guaranteed, if simultaneously

  (i) All production functions are strictly concave with respect to labor,

  (ii) $\lim\limits_{L_t \to 0} F_L(K_t,L_t,t+1) > w_t$,

(iii) $\lim_{L_t \to N_t} F_L(K_t, L_t, t+1) \leqq w_t$.

- In case of unique existence the optimal labor input L_t^* is strictly decreasing with respect to the wage rate w_t.

The latter will be assumed in the remainder of this section without further notice.

Now we turn to investigation of the workers' optimal wage policy given they know the capitalists' employment policy. As in Section 3.2, it is assumed that workers wish to maximize their utility from wage income according to assumption (A6.2).

Since it is assumed that workers know the capitalists' employment policy, each determination of the wage rate w_{t-1} actually is a determination of employment L_{t-1} according to

(3.7.4) $F_L(K_{t-1}, L_{t-1}, t) = w_{t-1}$, $t=1,..,T-1$.

Thus, if we assume that workers have full control over wages, we actually assume that they can control employment according to conditions (3.7.4). Therefore total wages in period t are given by

(3.7.7) $W_t = F_L(K_{t-1}, L_{t-1}, t) \cdot L_{t-1}$, $t=1,..,T$.

Due to the monotonicity of the utility function $U^W: \mathbb{R}^T \to \mathbb{R}$, maximization of utility from wage income is, again, equivalent to maximization of wages W_t in each period $t=1,..,T$. In period t the workers' problem is given by

$$\text{Maximize } F_L(K_{t-1}, L_{t-1}, t) L_{t-1}$$

(WP_t) subject to

$$0 < L_{t-1} \leqq N_{t-1}.$$

Simply as a matter of calculus we obtain the first and second order conditions for optimality

$$(3.7.8)\quad F_L(K_{t-1},L_{t-1},t) + F_{LL}(K_{t-1},L_{t-1},t)L_{t-1} = 0, \qquad t=1,..,T,$$

and

$$(3.7.9)\quad 2F_{LL}(K_{t-1},L_{t-1},t) + F_{LLL}(K_{t-1},L_{t-1},t)L_{t-1} < 0, \quad t=1,..,T.$$

For the general neo-classical production functions used so far neither of these conditions need to be satisfied. We therefore investigate the situation for several well-known neo-classical production functions in the remainder.

3.7.10 COBB-DOUGLAS PRODUCTION FUNCTIONS [1)]

For the following production functions

$$F(K_{t-1},L_{t-1},t) = c_t K_{t-1}^{b_t} L_{t-1}^{1-b_t}, \quad b_t \varepsilon (0,1), \quad c_t > 0, \quad t=1,..,T,$$

we obtain for all t=1,..,T

$$(3.7.11)\quad F_L(K_{t-1},L_{t-1},t)L_{t-1} = (1-b_t)F(K_{t-1},L_{t-1},t),$$

which is strictly increasing with respect to L_{t-1}.

As outlined above, by controlling the wage rate, workers can actually control employment according to conditions (3.7.4). The objective function (3.7.11) is strictly increasing with respect to L_{t-1}. Hence, for problem(WP_t) workers' optimal employment is given by

---

1) Here and in the remainder, only the linearly homogeneous forms of the production functions are considered. For the general Cobb-Douglas production function, however, it is trivially seen that results (3.7.12) and (3.7.13) hold, too.

(3.7.12) $L^*_{t-1} = N_{t-1}, \ t=1,..,T,$

and the corresponding optimal wage rates satisfy

(3.7.13) $F_L(K_{t-1},N_{t-1},t) = w^*_{t-1}, \ t=1,..,T.$

That is to say, if capitalists control employment according to wages then, for Cobb-Douglas production functions, workers' optimal wage policy leads to full employment. This holds for all problems (WP_t) i.e. for all periods t, t=1,..,T.

3.7.14 CES PRODUCTION FUNCTIONS

Consider the following productions functions

$$F(K_{t-1},L_{t-1},t) = c_t[\delta_t K_{t-1}^{\rho_t}+(1-\delta_t)L_{t-1}^{\rho_t}]^{1/\rho_t}, \ c_t>0,$$

$$\delta_t \varepsilon (0,1), \ 0 \neq \rho_t < 1, \ t=1,..,T.$$

Notice, the constant elasticity of substitution is given by

(3.7.15) $\sigma_t = 1/(1-\rho_t), \ t=1,..,T.$

If $\sigma_t > 1$, which implies $\rho_t \varepsilon (0,1)$, we see that for all t=1,..,T

(3.7.16) $F_L(K_{t-1},L_{t-1},t)L_{t-1} = c_t(1-\delta_t)[\delta_t K_{t-1}^{\rho_t}+(1-\delta_t)L_{t-1}^{\rho_t}]^{\frac{1-\rho_t}{\rho_t}} L_{t-1}^{\rho_t}$

is, again, strictly increasing with respect to L_{t-1}.[1)]

1) This result should not surprise because for $\sigma_t>1$ there exists some positive lower bound for marginal productivity of labor, name

$$F_L(K_{t-1},L_{t-1},t) > c(1-\delta)^{1/\rho}, t=1,..,T.$$

On the other hand, for $\sigma_t \varepsilon (0,1)$, there exists an upper bound

$$F_L(K_{t-1},L_{t-1},t) < c(1-\delta)^{1/\rho}, t=1,..,T.$$

Hence, in the first case wages are larger than $c(1-\delta)^{1/\rho}$ whereas in the second, they are smaller.

For $\sigma_t \to 1$ or, equivalently, $\rho_t \to 0$ the CES production function approaches the Cobb-Douglas production function above. Thus, for constant elasticities of substitution $\sigma_t \geqq 1$, capitalists' control over employment and workers' control over wages leads to full employment $L^*_{t-1} = N_{t-1}$ for all $t=1,..,T$. In these cases, problems (WP_t) have trivial solutions.

The other case of constant elasticity of substitution $\sigma_t \varepsilon (0,1)$ implying $\rho_t \varepsilon (-\infty,0)$ remains to be investigated.

Because of, for all t,

$$(3.7.17)\quad F_L(K_{t-1},L_{t-1},t) = c_t(1-\delta_t)[\delta_t K_{t-1}^{\rho_t} L_{t-1}^{-\rho_t} + (1-\delta_t)]^{\frac{1}{\rho_t}-1} \cdot$$

and

$$(3.7.18)\quad F_{LL}(K_{t-1},L_{t-1},t) = c_t(1-\delta_t)(\rho_t-1)\delta_t K_{t-1}^{\rho_t} L_{t-1}^{-\rho_t-1} \cdot [\delta_t K_{t-1}^{\rho_t} L_{t-1}^{\rho_t} + (1-\delta_t)]^{\frac{1}{\rho_t}-2}$$

we obtain from optimality conditions (3.7.8)

$$(3.7.19)\quad L^*_{t-1} = K_{t-1}[(-\delta_t \cdot \rho_t)/(1-\delta_t)]^{1/\rho_t}, \quad t=1,..,T.$$

That is, for sufficiently large N_{t-1}, there exists an interior extremum in the interval $(0,N_{t-1}]$. It is easy to show that for $\rho_t < 0$

$$(3.7.20)\quad F_{LL}(K_{t-1},L^*_{t-1},t) < 0, \qquad t=1,..,T.$$

Depending on the value of $\rho_t<0$, however, the product

$$(3.7.21)\quad F_{LLL}(K_{t-1},L_{t-1},t) \cdot L_{t-1}, \qquad t=1,..,T,$$

may be either positive or negative.

For given empirical production functions and parameter values it can easily be checked whether the second order conditions for optimality (3.7.9) hold or not. In the general case it does not matter so much, because all we can say is: *For* $\rho_t < 0$ *there may exists an interior solution to problem* (WP_t)*, that is, given capitalists' employment policy (3.7.4), for the workers a wage rate may be optimal although it leads to unemployment.* This result tells us that for a constant elasticity of substitution $\sigma_t \varepsilon (0,1)$ total wages are not necessarily maximized if we have full employment $L_t^* = N_t$ for all t. Thus, given capitalists employment policy, some unemployment is not a contradiction to workers' optimal control of wages.

3.7.22 GENERALIZED COBB DOUGLAS PRODUCTION FUNCTIONS

According to Diewert [1973], this production function is, for two inputs,

$$F(K_{t-1},L_{t-1},t) = c_t K_{t-1}^{b_t^1} L_{t-1}^{b_t^2} (K_{t-1}+L_{t-1})^{1-b_t^1-b_t^2},\quad c_t>0,$$

$$b_t^1, b_t^2 \varepsilon (0,1),\quad b_t^1+b_t^2 \leq 1,\qquad t=1,..,T.$$

As in the normal Cobb-Douglas case, we obtain here for all t, that the objective function is strictly increasing in labor:

$$\begin{aligned} & F_L(K_{t-1},L_{t-1},t)L_{t-1} = b_t^2 F(K_{t-1},L_{t-1},t) \\ (3.7.23)\quad & + c_t(1-b_t^1-b_t^2)K_{t-1}^{b_t^1}\left[K_{t-1}L_{t-1}^{-\frac{b_t^2+1}{b_t^1+b_t^2}} + L_{t-1}^{\frac{b_t^1-1}{b_t^1+b_t^2}}\right]^{-b_t^1-b_t^2} \end{aligned}$$

Notice that both exponents to L_{t-1} are negative.

Thus, here again, workers' optimal wages lead to full employment $L_{t-1}^* = N_{t-1}$, t=1,..,T.

We leave it to the reader to show that for the following Cobb-Douglas Generalization (in their neo-classical form) the same holds:

$$F(K_{t-1},L_{t-1},t) = c_t K_{t-1}^{b_t} L_{t-1}^{1-b_t} + g_t L_{t-1}, \quad c_t>0,\ g_t \geqq 0$$

(3.7.24)

$$b_t \varepsilon (0,1), \qquad t=1,..,T.$$

3.7.25 VES PRODUCTION FUNCTIONS

Finally in this section we consider the variable elasticity of substitution production function proposed by Revankar [1971]. The linearly homogeneous form is given by

$$F(K_{t-1},L_{t-1},t) = c_t K_{t-1}^{(1-\delta_t\rho_t)} [L_{t-1}+(\rho_t-1)K_{t-1}]^{\delta_t\rho_t},$$

$$c_t > 0,\ \delta_t \varepsilon (0,1),\ 0 \leqq \delta_t\rho_t \leqq 1,\ ^{1)}$$

$$L/K > (1-\rho_t)/(1-\delta_t\rho_t), \qquad t=1,..,T.$$

For this production function, the elasticity of substitution is

$$(3.7.26)\quad \sigma_t(K_{t-1},L_{t-1}) = 1+\frac{\rho_t-1}{1-\delta_t\rho_t}\frac{K_{t-1}}{L_{t-1}}, \qquad t=1,..,T.$$

The marginal product of labor is computed to be

$$F_L(K_{t-1},L_{t-1},t) = c_t \cdot \delta_t\rho_t K_{t-1}^{(1-\delta_t\rho_t)} \cdot$$

(3.7.27)

$$[L_{t-1}+(\rho_t-1)K_{t-1}]^{\delta_t\rho_t-1}, \quad t=1,..,T.$$

---

[1] Of course, Revankar should require $0<\delta_t\rho_t<1$, what will be assumed in the remainder.

Hence total wages $W_t = F_L(K_{t-1}, L_{t-1}, t)L_{t-1}$ are given by, for all t,

$$(3.7.28)\quad W_t = c\delta\rho K_{t-1}^{(1-\delta\rho)}[L_{t-1}^{\delta\rho/(\delta\rho-1)} + (\rho-1)K_{t-1}L_{t-1}^{1/(\delta\rho-1)}]^{\delta\rho-1}. \quad ^{1)}$$

Suppose we have $\rho_t \geqq 1$, i.e. $\sigma_t(K_{t-1}, L_{t-1}) \geqq 1$ for all t. Then it is easily checked that for the required range $0 < \delta_t\rho_t < 1$ W_t is strictly increasing with respect to L_{t-1}. Thus, like above for the CES, for Revankar's VES production function and $\sigma_t \geqq 1$ we also obtain full employment $L^*_{t-1} = N_{t-1}$, t=1,..,T, for the workers' optimal wage policy from problems (WP_t).

Now consider the other case of $\rho_t < 1$, i.e., the elasticity of substitution $\sigma_t(K_{t-1}, L_{t-1})$ is smaller than 1. As in the case of the CES production function we obtain that there may exist an interior extremum given by

$$(3.7.29)\quad L_{t-1} = K_{t-1}(1-\rho_t)/\delta_t\rho_t, \quad ^{2)} \qquad t=1,..,T.$$

Thus, again, for the workers a wage rate may be optimal which does not lead to full employment.

We sum up these results in the following theorem, which can now be stated without a proof.

3.7.30 THEOREM

Let the capitalists control employment according to Theorem (3.7.3) and suppose workers can control wages under full consideration of this policy. Then workers' optimal wage rate

---

[1] For simplicity the t-subscripts are omitted in this formula.

[2] Notice, because $L/K > (1-\rho_t)/(1-\delta_t\rho_t)$, L^*_{t-1} is in the feasible domain only for $\delta_t\rho_t < 1/2$.

w_t^* for all t is a full employment wage rate in the sense of

$$(3.7.31)\quad F(K_{t-1},N_{t-1},t) = w_{t-1}^*, \qquad t=1,..,T,$$

for each of the following productions functions:

a. Cobb-Douglas (3.7.10),

b. CES (3.7.14) with $\sigma_t \geqq 1$,

c. Generalized Cobb-Douglas (3.7.22) and (3.7.24),

d, VES (3.7.25) with $\sigma_t(K_{t-1},L_{t-1}) \geqq 1$.

In other words, if labor input is payed its marginal productivity, then the total wages are maximized at full employment $L_t = N_t$ for all the production functions above.

3.8 TAKING ACCOUNT OF THE STATE

So far in this work we have solely distinguished two groups in the society, namely workers and capitalists. While this may be justifiable for analyzing 18th or 19th century economies, it certainly limits the model's applicability to todays modern economies. It is the aim of this section, at least partially, to account for the state's role in economic life in taxing away part of each group's income and investing a fraction of it. Purposes and effects of taxes other than state's investment, however, are not considered here. We thus state the following assumption.

(A6) *Taxes and State's Investment*

In period t the state taxes away the fractions
(i) $\tau_t^w \in [0,1)$ of worker's income $W_t + D_t$,
(ii) $\tau_t^c \in [0,1]$ of capitalists' residual R_t.
Thus total taxes in each period t are given by

$$(3.8.1)\quad \tau_t^w(W_t + D_t) + \tau_t^c R_t \quad , \qquad t=1,..,T.$$

Out of the taxes obtained from workers the state invests the fraction $s_t^w \in [0,1]$ in period t, whereas from capitalists' taxes in period t, the fraction $s_t^c \in [0,1]$ is invested. State's total investment in period t is therefore given by

$$(3.8.2)\quad s_t^w \tau_t^w(W_t + D_t) + s_t^c \tau_t^c R_t \quad , \qquad t=1,..,T.$$

If in its investment plans the state does not distinguish from which source the corresponding taxes come one may assume $s_t^w = s_t^c$ for all t.

Assumptions (A1), (A2), (A4), and (A5) seem further adaequate for this section, whereas assumption (A3) needs to be modified. We substitute assumption (A3') for (A3).

(A3') *Saving and Investment*

The workers save and invest in period t of their net income after tax $(1-\tau_t^w)(W_t+D_t)$ the fraction $a_t \varepsilon [0,1)$. Capitalists invest the fraction $u_t \varepsilon [0,1]$ of their after tax residual $(1-\tau_t^c)R_t$ at time t. The state's investment is given by expression (3.8.2); thus total gross investment in period t is

$$I_t^g = a_t(1-\tau_t^w)(W_t+D_t) + u_t(1-\tau_t^c)R_t + \tag{3.8.3}$$
$$s_t^w \tau_t^w (W_t+D_t) + s_t^c \tau_t^c R_t \quad , \qquad t=1,..,T,$$

or, equivalently,

$$I_t^g = [a_t+(s_t^w-a_t)\tau_t^w](W_t+D_t) + \tag{3.8.4}$$
$$[u_t+(s_t^c-u_t)\tau_t^c]R_t \quad , \qquad t=1,..,T.$$

Notice that for $\tau_t^w = \tau_t^c = 0$ or $s_t^w = a_t$ and $s_t^c = u_t$ equations (3.8.4) reduce to (3.5). That is to say, if either taxes are zero or if the state invests of each group's tax liability the same proportion as the group itself would, then gross investment is the same as in the model without the state. Notice that the state is not assumed to receive direct income from its investments.

Due to assumptions (A3') and (A6), which are specific to this section, we need to modify deductions (D1) and (D2).

(D1') *Capital Development*

The capital stock in period t, K_t, is given by

$$K_t = [a_t+(s_t^w-a_t)\tau_t^w](W_t+D_t) + \tag{3.8.5}$$
$$[u_t+(s_t^c-u_t)\tau_t^c]R_t+(1-m_t)K_{t-1} \quad , \quad t=1,..,T,$$

or, equivalently,

$$K_t=[a_t+(s_t^w-a_t)\tau_t^w](w_{t-1}+d_{t-1})L_{t-1}+[u_t+(s_t^c-u_t)\tau_t^c]\cdot$$
(3.8.6)
$$[F(K_{t-1},L_{t-1},t)-(w_{t-1}+d_{t-1})L_{t-1}]+(1-m_t)K_{t-1}, t=1,..,T.$$

Thus, the investment ratio α_t in period t is

(3.8.7)
$$\alpha_t=u_t+(s_t^c-u_t)\tau_t^c-\frac{[u_t-a_t+(s_t^c-u_t)\tau_t^c-(s_t^w-a_t)\tau_t^w](w_{t-1}+d_{t-1})L_{t-1}}{F(K_{t-1},L_{t-1},t)},$$
$$t=1,..,T.$$

(D2') *Measurement of Workers' Share*

In addition to the shares β_t and γ_t defined in deduction (D2), in the model framework (A1),(A2),(A3'),(A4)-(A6), we work with workers' net share in period t, t=1,..,T, given by

(3.8.8) $$\gamma_t^n=(1-\tau_t^w)(w_{t-1}+d_{t-1})L_{t-1}/F(K_{t-1},L_{t-1},t), \quad t=1,..,T.$$

With K_t given by formula (3.8.5) or (3.8.6) and α_t given by formula (3.8.7), identities (3.12) and (3.13) from deduction (D3) hold for this section, too.

The first question to be analyzed in this section is whether or not the optimal investment policies for the cooperative case determined in Section 3.1 still apply in the model framework considered here. Thus we include assumption (A6.1) in our model framework of this section.

Inspection of problem (UP3.1) makes evident that for the cooperative case the modifications considered here do not matter. Therefore all the results from Section 3.1 still apply here.

Since that is not true for the results of Section 3.2, where workers control wages, this case will be investigated now.

3.8.1 WORKERS' CONTROL OF WAGES IN THE STATE MODEL

In addition to assumptions (A1),(A2),(A3'),(A4) through (A6), we now include the following assumption, which is a modification of assumption (A6.2) from Section 3.2 taking into account taxes on wages.

(A7.1) *Utility from Workers' Net Wages*

The group of workers is capable of assigning a value V to each possible sequence of total net wages $\{W_t^n\}_{t=1,..,T}$, where $W_t^n = (1-\tau_t^w)W_t$. Thus, for the workers there exists an aggregate utility function $U^w: \mathbb{R}^T \to \mathbb{R}$ with the usual properties,

$$(3.8.9)\quad V = U^w(W_1^n,\dots,W_T^n)\ .$$

Now the workers' problem is:

$$\text{(UP3.8.1)}\quad \begin{aligned} &\text{Maximize } U^w(W_1^n,\dots,W_T^n)\\ &\text{subject to}\\ &\left.\begin{aligned} &W_t^n=(1-\tau_t^w)w_{t-1}L_{t-1}\\ &K_t=[a_t+(s_t^w-a_t)\tau_t^w](w_{t-1}+d_{t-1})L_{t-1}+\\ &\quad[u_t+(s_t^c-u_t)\tau_t^c][F(K_{t-1},L_{t-1},t)-\\ &\quad(w_{t-1}+d_{t-1})L_{t-1}]+(1-m_t)K_{t-1} \end{aligned}\right\}\ t=1,..,T\\ &K_o,K_T>0 \text{ specified.} \end{aligned}$$

Notice, for

$$(3.8.9)\quad u_t+(s_t^c-u_t)\tau_t^c \leqq a_t+(s_t^w-a_t)\tau_t^w\ ,\qquad t=1,..,T,$$

the dynamic equation for K_t is nondecreasing with respect to

w_{t-1}. The left-hand-side of inequality (3.8.9) is the effective investment share per unit of capitalists' residual before tax, whereas the right-hand-side constitutes the fraction of effective investment per unit workers' income before tax. Thus inequality (3.8.9) states that effective investment per unit of capitalists' residual is not larger than that per unit of workers' income. Clearly, if this holds, then workers may increase their wage rate and therefore their utility without decreasing the subsequent capital stock. Obviously, it is then optimal for them to set wages such that

$$(3.8.10) \quad W_t = F(K_{t-1},L_{t-1},t) - D_t \quad , \qquad t=1,..,T.$$

That is to say, capitalists' residual reduces to zero and workers' income before tax is equal to total output. Thus, when inequalities (3.8.9) hold, problem (3.8.1) is trivially solved.

Hence, the interesting case to be investigated here is when effective investment of capitalists is larger than the one of workers, i.e., we have

$$(3.8.11) \quad u_t+(s_t^c-u_t)\tau_t^c > a_t+(s_t^w-a_t)\tau_t^w \quad , \qquad t=1,..,T.$$

For this case we state the following theorem, which is similar to Theorem 3.2.3 and can be derived and proved the same way.

<u>3.8.12 Theorem</u>

Let the assumptions (A1),(A2),(A3'),(A4) through (A6) and (A7.1) as well as inequalities (3.8.11) hold for problem (UP3.8.1). If there exists a feasible[1] sequence of capital stocks $\{K_t^*\}_{t=0,..,T}$ satisfying the equation system

---

[1] See footnotes 1) from page 25and page 30.

(3.8.13)
$$F_K(K_{t-1},L_{t-1},t) = \left[\left(\frac{\partial U^w}{\partial W^n_{t-1}}\middle|\frac{\partial U^w}{\partial W^n_t}\right)\frac{1-\tau^w_{t-1}}{1-\tau^w_t}\cdot\right.$$
$$\left.\frac{a_t - u_t + (s^w_t - a_t)\tau^w_t - (s^c_t - u_t)\tau^c_t}{a_{t-1}-u_{t-1}+(s^w_{t-1}-a_{t-1})\tau^w_{t-1}-(s^c_{t-1}-u_{t-1})\tau^c_{t-1}} + m_t - 1\right] / [u_t+(s^c_t-u_t)\tau^c_t],$$

t=2,..,T,

then it constitutes a sequence of optimal capital stocks for problem (UP3.8.1). The sequence of optimal wage rates $\{w^*_t\}_{t=0,..,T-1}$ is given by

(3.8.14)
$$w^*_t = \frac{[u_{t+1}+(s^c_{t+1}-u_{t+1})\tau^c_{t+1}]F(K^*_t,L_t,t+1)+(1-m_{t+1})K^*_t-K^*_{t+1}}{L_t[u_{t+1}-a_{t+1}-(s^w_{t+1}-a_{t+1})\tau^w_{t+1}+(s^c_{t+1}-u_{t+1})\tau^c_{t+1}]} - d_t,$$

t=0,..,T-1.

Note that if all tax rates are zero the results (3.8.13) and (3.8.14) reduce to (3.2.4.) and (3.2.5), respectively. If all tax and saving parameters are constant in time, we have

(3.8.15)
$$F_K(K_{t-1},L_{t-1},t) = \frac{\left(\frac{U^w}{W^n_{t-1}}\middle|\frac{U^w}{W^n_t}\right) + m_t - 1}{u + (s^c - u)\tau^c}, \quad t=1,..,T.$$

Thus result (3.8.13) can significantly be simplified if we give up the assumption of all parameters depending on time. It is further simplified if workers wish to maximize the present values of wages after tax instead of maximizing utility. Then we obtain the optimality conditions

(3.8.16)
$$F_K(K_{t-1},L_{t-1},t) = (i_{t-1}+m_t)/[u+(s^c-u)\tau^c], \quad t=1,..,T.$$

Comparison of these conditions with the corresponding ones of the cooperative case and the model without state (3.1.20) and (3.2.11) makes the following remarks straightforward.

3.8.17 Remarks

Recall u, $s^c, \tau^c \in [0,1]$.

(i) Optimality conditions (3.1.20) and (3.8.16) are equivalent if and only if $u+(s^c-u)\tau^c = 1$. Thus the same optimal capital stocks as in the cooperative case are obtained here in each of the following situations:

- $u = s^c = 1$, i.e., both capitalists and the state invest maximally. Then the tax rate on capitalists' residual income τ^c does not matter.
- $s^c = \tau^c = 1$, i.e., government taxes away all capitalists' residual and invests all of it. Then the capitalists' (hypothetical) investment rate u does not matter.
- $u = 1$, $\tau^c = 0$, i.e., capitalists invest maximally and government imposes no tax on their residual income. Then government's (hypothetical) investment rate from capitalists' taxes s^c does not matter.

(ii) Optimality conditions (3.2.11) for $u_t = u$ and (3.8.16) are equivalent if and only if $(s^c-u)\tau^c = 0$. Thus the same capital stocks are optimal in the models with and without state if at least one of the following situations holds:

- $s^c = u$, i.e., government invests the same proportion of the taxes obtained from capitalists as capitalists themselves. Then the tax rate τ^c does not matter.
- $\tau^c = 0$, i.e., government imposes no tax on capitalists residual income.

We conclude this paragraph by deriving a few results for the case of all parameters and the production function being constant in time. Marginal productivity of the per capita capital stocks satisfying the optimality conditions agrees with (3.8.16). The investment ratio, derived similarly to result (3.2.23), is given by

$$(3.8.18)\quad \alpha_t=\alpha=\eta(k^*)[u+(s^c-u)\tau^c](l+m)/(i+m)\quad ,\quad t=2,..,T-1,$$

where $\eta(k^*)$ is the capital elasticity of output of the optimal capital stock.

For the workers' share in output, it follows by linear homogeneity for the case considered

$$(3.8.19)\quad \gamma_t=\gamma=[1-\eta(k^*)\frac{l+m}{i+m}]/[1-\frac{a+(s^w-a)\tau^w}{u+(s^c-u)\tau^c}]\quad ,\quad t=2,..,T-1.$$

Notice, this result agrees with the corresponding one from Section 3.2, (3.2.25),for $\tau^w=\tau^c=0$. Workers' net share, defined in deduction (D2'), thus is

$$(3.8.20)\quad \gamma_t^n=(1-\tau^w)[1-\eta(k^*)\frac{l+m}{i+m}]/[1-\frac{a+(s^w-a)\tau^w}{u+(s^c-u)\tau^c}],\ t=2,..,T-1.$$

We leave it to the reader to investigate the impact of different parameter values on workers' (optimal) shares. It has to be taken into account, however, that except for the Cobb-Douglas production function, $\eta(k^*)$ depends on the parameters i,m,u,s^c, and τ^c,too.

3.8.21 Example

Assume the numerical values from Example 3.2.26 $\eta(k^*) = 0.3$, $m = 0.1$, $i = 0.05$, $l = 0.02$, $u = 0.75$, $a = 0.04$, and, in addition, $s^w=s^c=0.5$, $\tau^c=0.6$, $\tau^w=0.1$. Then equation (3.1.28) yielded the cooperative optimal investment ratio $\alpha^*= 0.24$. If workers have full control over wages, their optimal shares are given by $\gamma= 0.887$ and $\gamma^n= 0.798$ approximately. The corresponding investment ratio is $\alpha= 0.144$ (exactly), i.e. 40 % below the optimal one.

3.8.2 CAPITALISTS' CONTROL OF INVESTMENT IN THE STATE MODEL

According to assumptions (A3') and (A6), the consumable part of capitalists'after tax residual is given by

$$(3.8.22)\quad R_t^A = (1-u_t)(1-\tau_t^c)R_t \quad , \qquad t=1,..,T.$$

Of the capitalists'total residual R_t, the state invests $s_t^c\tau_t^c R_t$ and capitalists invest $u_t(1-\tau_t^c)R_t$.

In addition to assumptions (A1),(A2),(A3'),(A4) through (A6), we now include a modification of assumption (A6.3) taking into account capitalists' tax liability.

(A7.2) *Utility from Capitalists' Consumption*

The group of capitalists is capable of assigning a value V to each possible sequence of consumable residuals (after tax) $\{R_t^A\}_{t=1,..,T}$. There exists an aggregate utility function $U^A: \mathbb{R}^T \to \mathbb{R}$

$$(3.8.23)\quad V = U^A(R_1^A,..,R_T^A)$$

with the usual properties.

In the presence of the state, the capitalists problem is:

Maximize $U^A(R_1^A,..,R_T^A)$

subject to

$$(\text{UP}3.8.2)\quad \left.\begin{aligned} R_t^A &= (1-u_t)(1-\tau_t^c)[F(K_{t-1},L_{t-1},t)-(w_{t-1}+d_{t-1})L_{t-1}] \\ K_t &= [u_t(1-\tau_t^c)+s_t^c\tau_t^c][F(K_{t-1},L_{t-1},t)-(w_{t-1}+d_{t-1})L_{t-1}]+ \\ &\quad [a_t(1-\tau_t^w)+s_t^w\tau_t^w](w_{t-1}+d_{t-1})L_{t-1}+(1-m_t)K_{t-1}\ , \end{aligned}\right\} t=1,..,T,$$

$K_o, K_T > 0$ specified.

Notice that, with respect to the control variable u_t, R_t^A is a nonincreasing function while the dynamic equation for K_t is nondecreasing. Problem (UP3.8.2) is again a special problem (UP) from Chapter 6 with conditions (IA) satisfied. We thus apply Theorem 6.1 and obtain:

3.8.24 Theorem

Let the assumptions (A1),(A2),(A3'),(A4) through (A6) and (A7.2) hold for problem (UP3.8.2) and $\tau_t^c \in [0,1)$. If there exists a feasible sequence of capital stocks $\{K_t^*\}_{t=0,..,T}$ satisfying the equation system

$$(3.8.25)\quad F_K(K_{t-1},L_{t-1},t)=\frac{\left[\frac{\partial U^A}{\partial R_{t-1}^A}\middle|\frac{\partial U^A}{\partial R_t^A}\right]+m_t-1}{1-\tau_t^c(1-s_t^c)},\qquad t=2,..,T,$$

then it constitutes a sequence of optimal capital stocks for problem (UP3.8.2). The sequence of optimal investment rates $\{u_t^*\}_{t=1,..,T}$ is given by

$$(3.8.26)\quad u_t^*=\frac{K_t^*-(1-m_t)K_{t-1}^*-[a_t(1-\tau_t^w)+s_t^w\tau_t^w](w_{t-1}+d_{t-1})L_{t-1}}{(1-\tau_t^c)[F(K_{t-1}^*,L_{t-1},t)-(w_{t-1}+d_{t-1})L_{t-1}]}-\frac{s_t^c\tau_t^c}{1-\tau_t^c},\ t=1,..,T.$$

Notice, because of $\tau_t^c \in [0,1)$ and $s_t^c \in [0,1]$ all denominators in equations (3.8.25) and (3.8.26) are guaranteed to be positive. For $\tau_t^c=0$ or $s_t^c=1$ the denominators of equations (3.8.25) are equal to 1. Thus, if the corresponding ratios of marginal utilities are identical, then optimality conditions (3.8.25) check with (3.3.2), the corresponding conditions from the model without state.

If capitalists seek to maximize the present value of their consumable residuals after tax instead of utility and all parameters are constant in time, we obtain from optimality conditions (3.8.13)

$$(3.8.27)\quad F_K(K_{t-1},L_{t-1},t) = (i+m)/(1-\tau^c+\tau^c s^c) \quad , \qquad t=2,..,T.$$

Thus the same capital stocks are optimal in the models with and without the state, if either the tax rate τ^c is zero or government's investment rate s^c is equal to 1.

Comparing results (3.8.16) and (3.8.27), we obtain the same result as in the models without state (see Section 3.4, result (3.4.10)). Only for $u=1$, i.e. capitalists investing all of their residual income, both optimality conditions are equivalent. Thus the resulting investment ratios are identical for this case, too, as a comparison of result (3.8.18) with the following result shows

$$(3.8.28)\quad \alpha_t=\alpha=\eta(k^*)(1-\tau^c+\tau^c s^c)(1+m)/(i+m) \quad , \qquad t=2,..,T-1.$$

This result is obtained by multiplying the right-hand-side of equations (3.1.25), which also apply here, with

$$f'(k^*)\frac{i+m}{1-\tau^c+\tau^c s^c} = 1$$

Capitalists' optimal investment rate, constant in time from period 2 through T-1 as well, is given by

$$(3.8.29)\quad u_t^*=u^*=\frac{(1+m)k^*-[a(1-\tau^w)+s^w\tau^w](w+d)}{(1-\tau^c)(f(k^*)-w-d)}-\frac{s^c\tau^c}{1-\tau^c} \quad , \qquad t=2,..,T-1,$$

as is easily derived from result (3.8.26) for the case considered. For the workers' share in output, we obtain

$$(3.8.30)\quad \gamma_t=\gamma=[1-\eta(k^*)\frac{1+m}{i+m}\frac{1-\tau^c+\tau^c s^c}{u-u\tau^c+\tau^c s^c}]/[1-\frac{a+(s^w-a)\tau^w}{u+(s^c-u)\tau^c}] \quad , \qquad t=2,..,T-1.$$

Notice, for $\tau^c=\tau^w=0$, this result agrees with the corresponding one from Section 3.3, (3.3.20).

Since $\gamma_t^n = (1-\tau^w)\gamma_t$, workers' net share is given by

$$(3.8.31)\quad \gamma_t^n = \gamma = (1-\tau^w)\,[1 - \eta(k^*)\frac{i+m}{i+m}\,\frac{1-\tau^c+\tau^c s^c}{u-u\tau^c+\tau^c s^c}]\ /$$

$$[1 - \frac{a+(s^w-a)\tau^w}{u+(s^c-u)\tau^c}] \quad , \qquad t=2,..,T-1.$$

3.8.32 Example

Let the production function be constant in time and given by

$$(3.8.33)\quad F(K_{t-1},L_{t-1},t) = \frac{cK_{t-1}L_{t-1}}{b_1K_{t-1}+b_2L_{t-1}}\ ,\ c,b_1,b_2 > 0,\quad t=1,..,T.$$

Then the per capita production function, also constant in time, is given by

$$(3.8.34)\quad f(k_{t-1}) = \frac{ck_{t-1}}{b_1k_{t-1} + b_2} \quad , \qquad t=1,..,T.$$

Notice that this production function is, in fact, strictly increasing and concave for $k_{t-1} > 0$. The time constant per capita capital stock, which is optimal for the capitalists, is obtained from the following optimality conditions

$$(3.8.35)\quad f'(k_{t-1}) = (i+m)/(1-\tau^c+\tau^c s^c) \quad , \qquad t=2,..,T,$$

namely,

$$(3.8.36)\quad k_t^* = k^* = \frac{1}{b_1}\left[\frac{cb_2(1-\tau^c+\tau^c s^c)}{i + m}\right]^{1/2} - \frac{b_2}{b_1} \quad , \qquad t=1,..,T-1.$$

The capital elasticity of output is computed to be

$$(3.8.37)\quad \eta(k^*) = \left[\frac{b_2(i+m)}{c(1-\tau^c+\tau^c s^c)}\right]^{1/2} \quad .$$

From equations (3.8.29) we obtain the capitalists' optimal investment rate

$$(3.8.38)\quad u^{*}=\frac{\frac{l+m}{b_1}(\sqrt{\ }-b_2)-[a(1-\tau^{w})+s^{w}\tau^{w}](w+d)}{\frac{c(1-\tau^{c})}{b_1}(1-\frac{b_2}{\sqrt{\ }})-(1-\tau^{c})(w+d)}-\frac{s^{c}\tau^{c}}{1-\tau^{c}}\;,t=2,..,T-1,$$

where

$$\sqrt{\ }=\left[\frac{cb_2(1-\tau^{c}+\tau^{c}s^{c})}{i+m}\right]^{1/2}.$$

The corresponding investment ratio is given by

$$(3.8.39)\quad \alpha=\eta(k^{*})(l+m)\left[\frac{b_2(1-\tau^{c}+\tau^{c}s^{c})}{c(i+m)}\right]^{1/2},\qquad t=2,..,T-1.$$

We now insert the following realistic values in the formulas above: $m=0.1$, $i=0.05$, $l=0.02$, $a=0.04$, $s^{w}=s^{c}=0.5$, $\tau^{c}=0.6$, $\tau^{w}=0.1$, $c=b_1=b_2=1$, $w=0.2$, $d=0.1$.
Then the optimal per capita capital stock is computed to be $k^{*}=1.16$, per capita output $f(k^{*})=0.0537$. By using formulas (3.8.29) or (3.8.38) it is easily veryfied that the capitalists' optimal investment rate is $u^{*}=0.446$. The corresponding investment ratio from formula (3.8.39) is computed to be $\alpha\cong 0.26$, whereas the cooperative optimal one in our example is from formula (3.1.28) $\alpha^{*}=0.31$, i.e. 31 %. This value is obtained by noting that in the cooperative case the optimal capital stock is $k^{*}\cong 1.582$ and thus $\eta(k^{*})\cong 0.387$.

Notice here again that the cooperative optimal values can be obtained from the formulas above by letting $\tau^{c}=0$ or $s^{c}=1$. We now compute the workers' shares for the case when capitalists control investment either by formulas (3.8.30) or directly from the values above and obtain $\gamma\cong 0.559$ and $\gamma^{n}\cong 0.503$.

3.8.3 Conclusions

It was the purpose of this section to show how we can take account of the state in the model framework analyzed so far. Some of the important results from Sections 3.1 through 3.3 have thus been generalized here. A generalization of the results from Sections 3.4 through 3.7 can be done similarly as indicated above. For reasons of space, however, this exercise is left to the interested reader.

Our conclusion is that the model can in fact be extended to account for the presence of the state taxing away part of each groups' income and investing a fraction of it. We have not investigated, however, purposes and effects of taxes other than investment.

3.9 SOME EXTENSIONS AND LIMITATIONS OF THE MODEL

So far, in analyzing the model of distribution and wealth, workers' dividend income was accounted for by exogeneous variables only. We thus have neglected that workers' capital income should depend on their prior saving and investment behavior. This dependance is, of course, closely related to their partial ownership of the economy's capital stock.

In economic reality, there is no doubt that, via their saving and investment, workers have several opportunities to own part of the capital stock and receive capital income accordingly. When introducing Machaczek's [1984] model in Section 2.4, it was briefly discussed already that it is important to distinguish between capitalists' and workers' capital stocks and it seems reasonable to assume that the residual capital income is distributed according to capital ownership. This will be incorporated in our model framework now. The assumptions will therefore be modified in the following way:

(A 9.1) *Production*

The economy's GNP in period t is given by

(3.9.1) $Y_t = F(K^c_{t-1} + K^w_{t-1}, L_{t-1}, t)$, $t = 1,..,T$,

where K^c_{t-1} and K^w_{t-1} denote the capitalists' and workers' capital stock shares from period t-1, respectively. The production function $F: \mathbb{R}^2_+ \times \mathbb{N} \to \mathbb{R}_+$ is again assumed nondecreasing, concave, continuously differentiable twice and linearly homogeneous. In period t, capital of period t-1 is depreciated with rate $m_t \varepsilon [0,1]$.

(A 9.2) *Distribution*

In each period t, total wages are given by

(3.9.2) $W_t = w_{t-1} L_{t-1}$, $t = 1,..,T$,

residual capital income is therefore

(3.9.3) $F(K^c_{t-1}+K^w_{t-1},L_{t-1},t) - w_{t-1}L_{t-1}$, $t=1,..,T.$

According to their capital stock shares, workers receive

(3.9.4) $$D_t = \frac{K^w_{t-1}}{K^c_{t-1}+K^w_{t-1}} [F(K^c_{t-1}+K^w_{t-1},L_{t-1},t)-w_{t-1}L_{t-1}], t=1,..,T,$$

and capitalists receive

(3.9.5) $$R_t = \frac{K^c_{t-1}}{K^c_{t-1}+K^w_{t-1}} [F(K^c_{t-1}+K^w_{t-1},L_{t-1},t)-w_{t-1}L_{t-1}], t=1,..,T.$$

(A 9.3) = (A 3), but later $a^w_t = a^d_t$ or $u_t = 1$ will be required.

(A 9.4) = (A 4)

(A 9.5) *Boundary Condition*

In period $t=0$, the groups in the economy start with capital stocks $K^w_o > 0$ and $K^c_o > 0$, respectively.

We start with considering

3.9.1 WORKERS CONTROLLING WAGES WHEN DIVIDENDS ARE ENDOGENEOUS

(A 9.6) *Objective*

Workers seek to maximize the present value of their consumption, i.e. net income after saving.

(3.9.6) $$\text{Maximize} \sum_{t=1}^{T} N^w_t \prod_{j=0}^{t-1} (1+i_j)^{-1} ,$$

where

(3.9.7) $$N^w_t = (1-a^w_t)w_{t-1}L_{t-1} + (1-a^d_t)\frac{K^w_{t-1}}{K^c_{t-1}+K^w_{t-1}} \cdot [F(K^c_{t-1}+K^w_{t-1},L_{t-1},t) - w_{t-1}L_{t-1}] , \quad t=1,..,T.$$

From these assumptions we deduce that both groups' capital stock shares are given by

$$(3.9.8)\quad K_t^c = \frac{u_t K_{t-1}^c}{K_{t-1}^c + K_{t-1}^w}\left[F(K_{t-1}^c + K_{t-1}^w, L_{t-1}, t) - w_{t-1}L_{t-1}\right] + (1-m_t)K_{t-1}^c, \quad t=1,..,T,$$

and

$$(3.9.9)\quad \begin{aligned} K_t^w = {} & \frac{a_t^d K_{t-1}^w}{K_{t-1}^c + K_{t-1}^w}\left[F(K_{t-1}^c + K_{t-1}^w, L_{t-1}, t) - w_{t-1}L_{t-1}\right] + a_t^w w_{t-1}L_{t-1} \\ & + (1-m_t)K_{t-1}^w, \qquad t=1,..,T, \end{aligned}$$

such that

$$(3.9.10)\quad \begin{aligned} K_t^c + K_t^w = {} & \frac{u_t K_{t-1}^c + a_t^d K_{t-1}^w}{K_{t-1}^c + K_{t-1}^w}\left[F(K_{t-1}^c + K_{t-1}^w, L_{t-1}, t) - w_{t-1}L_{t-1}\right] \\ & + a_t^w w_{t-1}L_{t-1} + (1-m_t)(K_{t-1}^c + K_{t-1}^w), \qquad t=1,..,T. \end{aligned}$$

The following optimization shows as an example, that such a slight modification can make a problem considerably harder. Formally, the problem is:

$$\text{Maximize} \sum_{t=1}^{T} \left[(1-a_t^w) w_{t-1}L_{t-1} + (1-a_t^d)\frac{K_{t-1}^w}{K_{t-1}^c + K_{t-1}^w} \cdot \left[F(K_{t-1}^c + K_{t-1}^w, L_{t-1}, t) - w_{t-1}L_{t-1}\right]\right] \prod_{j=0}^{t-1}(1+i_j)^{-1}$$

subject to

$$(P3.9)\quad \begin{aligned} K_t^c = {} & \frac{u_t K_{t-1}^c}{K_{t-1}^c + K_{t-1}^w}\left[F(K_{t-1}^c + K_{t-1}^w, L_{t-1}, t) - w_{t-1}L_{t-1}\right] + (1-m_t)K_{t-1}^c, \\ K_t^w = {} & \frac{a_t^d K_{t-1}^w}{K_{t-1}^c + K_{t-1}^w}\left[F(K_{t-1}^c + K_{t-1}^w, L_{t-1}, t) - w_{t-1}L_{t-1}\right] \qquad (t=1,..,T) \\ & + a_t^w w_{t-1}L_{t-1} + (1-m_t)K_{t-1}^w, \end{aligned}$$

$K_0^w, K_0^c > 0$ specified

Problem (P3.9) is trivial if $u_t \leq a_t^w$ as was discussed earlier. Thus we require $u_t > a_t^w$ for all t. If we attack problem (P3.9) by means of standard dynamic programming, where $\Phi_t(K_{t-1}^c, K_{t-1}^w)$ denotes the recurrence relation on stage t, we obtain for T:

$$(3.9.11) \quad \Phi_T(K_{T-1}^c, K_{T-1}^w) = \underset{w_{T-1}}{\text{Max}} \{N_T^w\} ,$$

where N_T^w is given by formula (3.9.7) for t=T. For

$$(3.9.12) \quad (1-a_T^w)/(1-a_T^d) > K_{T-1}^w/(K_{T-1}^c+K_{T-1}^w)$$

N_T^w is strictly increasing with respect to w_{T-1}. Condition (3.9.12) will be satisfied for $a_T^w = a_T^d$, which will be partially required later. In any case, positive saving and investment does not make sense for the workers in period T, hence it would be quite realistic to require $a_T^w = a_T^d = 0$ implying condition (3.9.12) holds. Due to the monotonicity mentioned above the optimal wage rate in period T-1 is

$$(3.9.13) \quad w_{T-1}^* = F(K_{T-1}^c+K_{T-1}^w, L_{T-1}, T)/L_T$$

and hence

$$(3.9.14) \quad \Phi_T(K_{T-1}^c, K_{T-1}^w) = (1-a_T^w)F(K_{T-1}^c+K_{T-1}^w, L_{T-1}, T) =: \Phi_T$$ [1)]

which only depends on the sum $K_{T-1}^c+K_{T-1}^w$. On stage T-1, we have

$$(3.9.15) \quad \Phi_{T-1} = \underset{w_{T-2}}{\text{Max}} \{N_{T-1}^w + (1+i_{T-1})^{-1}\Phi_T\}$$

where Φ_T can be expressed as a function of K_{T-2}^c and K_{T-2}^w by using formulas (3.9.8) and (3.9.9). As an optimality condition we obtain by differentiation of $\{N_{T-1}^w+(1+i_{T-1})^{-1}\Phi_T\}$ with respect to w_{T-2}:

---

1) The recurrence relations' arguments are omitted further to simplify notation.

$$F_K\left(\frac{u_{T-1}K^c_{T-2}+a^d_{T-1}K^w_{T-2}}{K^c_{T-2}+K^w_{T-2}}\,[F(K^c_{T-2}+K^w_{T-2},L_{T-2},T-1)-w_{T-2}L_{T-2}]\right.$$

$$(3.9.16)\quad \left.+a^w_{T-1}w_{T-2}L_{T-2}+(1-m_{T-1})(K^c_{T-2}+K^w_{T-2}),L_{T-1},T\right) \overset{!}{=}$$

$$\frac{1+i_{T-1}}{1-a^w_T}\;\frac{(a^w_{T-1}-a^d_{T-1})K^w_{T-2}-(1-a^w_{T-1})K^c_{T-2}}{(a^w_{T-1}-a^d_{T-1})K^w_{T-2}-(u_{T-1}-a^w_{T-1})K^c_{T-2}} \quad =: c_{T-1}$$

Due to concavity, this and the following first order conditions are sufficient for a maximum. Thus, if the inverse of period T's production function capital derivative, denoted by $F^{-1}_{K,T}$, exists, the optimal control is given by

$$w^*_{T-2}(K^c_{T-2},K^w_{T-2}) = [F^{-1}_{K,T}(c_{T-1}) - (1-m_{T-1})(K^c_{T-2}+K^w_{T-2}) -$$

$$(3.9.17)\quad \frac{u_{T-1}K^c_{T-2}+a^d_{T-1}K^w_{T-2}}{K^c_{T-2}+K^w_{T-2}}\,F(K^c_{T-2}+K^w_{T-2},L_{T-2},T-1)\;]\;/\;[\;a^w_{T-1}L_{T-2}$$

$$-\;\frac{u_{T-1}K^c_{T-2}+a^d_{T-1}K^w_{T-2}}{K^c_{T-2}+K^w_{T-2}}\cdot L_{T-2}\;].$$

With this optimal control, we notice that

$$(3.9.18)\quad F_K(K^c_{T-1}+K^{w\,*}_{T-1},L_{T-1},T) = c_{T-1}$$

does not depend on K^c_{T-2} or K^w_{T-2} for $a^d_{T-1} = a^w_{T-1} = a_{T-1}$. In this case we have

$$(3.9.19)\quad F_K(K^c_{T-1}+K^{w\,*}_{T-1},L_{T-1},T) = \frac{1-a_{T-1}}{1-a_T}\;\frac{1+i_{T-1}}{u_{T-1}-a_{T-1}} \quad .$$

Thus the optimal total capital stock is independent of the preceding capital stocks.

Inserting the optimal policy (3.9.17) into the recurrence relation from stage T-1, we have for $a^w_{T-1} = a^d_{T-1} = a_t$:

$$\Phi_{T-1} = \frac{1-a_{T-1}}{u_{T-1}-a_{T-1}} [F(K^C_{T-2}+K^W_{T-2}, L_{T-2}, T-1) + (1-m_{T-1})(K^C_{T-2}+K^W_{T-2}) -$$

(3.9.20)

$$F^{-1}_{K,T}(\frac{1-a_{T-1}}{1-a_T}\frac{1+i_{T-1}}{u_{T-1}-a_{T-1}})] + \frac{1-a_T}{1+i_{T-1}} F(F^{-1}_{K,T}(\frac{1-a_{T-1}}{1-a_T}\frac{1+i_{T-1}}{u_{T-1}-a_{T-1}}), L_{T-1}, T)$$

which, again, only depends on the sum $K^C_{T-2}+K^W_{T-2}$.

For $a^W_{T-1} \neq a^d_{T-1}$ we obtain lengthy formulas and quite intractable results for $t < T-1$. Thus, in the remainder of this derivation we assume $a^W_t = a^d_t = a_t$ for all $t \leqq T$ without further notice.

On stage T-2 we have

$$\text{(3.9.21)} \quad \Phi_{T-2} = \underset{w_{T-3}}{\text{Max}} \{ N^W_{T-2} + (1+i_{T-2})^{-1}\Phi_{T-1} \} ,$$

where Φ_{T-1} may be expressed as a function of $K^C_{T-3}+K^W_{T-3}$. By determination of $w^*_{T-3}(K^C_{T-3}, K^C_{T-3})$ and insertion of the result into the optimality condition, we obtain

$$\text{(3.9.22)} \quad F_K(K^C_{T-2}+K^{W*}_{T-2}, L_{T-2}, T-1) = \frac{1}{u_{T-1}}\left[\frac{1-a_{T-2}}{1-a_{T-1}}\frac{u_{T-1}-a_{T-1}}{u_{T-2}-a_{T-2}}(1+i_{T-2})+m_{T-1}-1\right]$$

which, again, is independent of the preceding capital stocks. Notice, for $u_{T-1}=u_{T-2}=1$, we obtain from formula (3.9.22)

$$F_K(K^C_{T-2}+K^{W*}_{T-2}, L_{T-2}, T-1) = i_{T-2}+m_{T-1} .$$

We will return to that case later.

On stage T-2 we obtain the recurrence relation

$$\Phi_{T-2} = \frac{1-a_{T-2}}{u_{T-2}-a_{T-2}} [F(K^C_{T-3}+K^W_{T-3}, L_{T-3}, T-2) + (1-m_{T-2})(K^C_{T-3}+K^W_{T-3}) -$$

(3.9.23)

$$\underbrace{F^{-1}_{K,T-1}(\frac{1}{u_{T-1}}\left[\frac{1-a_{T-2}}{1-a_{T-1}}\frac{u_{T-1}-a_{T-1}}{u_{T-2}-a_{T-2}}(1+i_{T-2}) + m_{T-1}-1\right])}_{=:c_{T-2}}] + (1+i_{T-2})^{-1}\Phi_{T-1},$$

where Φ_{T-1} from formula (3.9.20) only depends on

(3.9.24) $K^c_{T-2}+K^{w\,*}_{T-2} = F^{-1}_{K,T-1}(c_{T-2})$

and

(3.9.25) $K^c_{T-1}+K^{w\,*}_{T-1} = F^{-1}_{K,T}(c_{T-1})$.

Proceeding further in backward dynamic programming, one can show by induction after considerable computational effort

$$(3.9.26)\quad F_K(K^c_{t-1}+K^{w\,*}_{t-1},L_{t-1},t) = \frac{1}{u_t}\left[\frac{1-a_{t-1}}{1-a_t}\,\frac{u_t-a_t}{u_{t-1}-a_{t-1}}(1+i_{t-1})+m_t-1\right], t=2,..,T-1$$

We have thus derived the following

<u>3.9.27 Theorem</u>

Let the assumptions (A 9.1) through (A 9.6) and $a^w_t = a^d_t = a_t < u_t$ for all t be satisfied for problem (P3.9). If there exists a feasible sequence of workers' capital stocks $\{K^{w*}_t\}_{t=0,..,T'}$ satisfying the equations

$$(3.9.28)\quad F_K(K^c_{t-1}+K^w_{t-1},L_{t-1},t) = \frac{1}{u_t}\left[\frac{1-a_{t-1}}{1-a_t}\,\frac{u_t-a_t}{u_{t-1}-a_{t-1}}(1+i_{t-1})+m_t-1\right], t=2,..,T-1$$

and

$$(3.9.29)\quad F_K(K^c_{t-1}+K^w_{t-1},L_{t-1},t) = \frac{1-a_{T-1}}{1-a_T}\,\frac{1+i_{T-1}}{u_{T-1}-a_{T-1}} \qquad t=T,$$

then $\{K^{w*}_t\}_{t=0,..,T}$ constitutes a sequence of optimal workers' capital stocks for problem (P3.9). The sequence of optimal wages $\{w^*_t\}_{t=0,..,T-1}$ is given by

$$(3.9.30)\quad w^*_t = [K^c_{t+1}+K^{w\,*}_{t+1}-(1-m_{t+1})(K^c_t+K^{w*}_t) - \frac{u_{t+1}K^c_t+a^d_{t+1}K^{w*}_t}{K^c_t+K^{w*}_t}\,.$$
$$F(K^c_t+K^{w*}_t,L_t,t+1)\,]\,/\,[\,a^w_{t+1} - \frac{u_{t+1}K^c_t+a^d_{t+1}K^{w*}_t}{K^c_t+K^{w*}_t}\,]\,L_t,\ t=0,..,T-1.$$

When deriving Theorem 3.9.27's result we have used the condition $a_t^d = a_t^w = a_t$ guaranteeing tractability. Instead, the (restrictive) condition $u_t = 1$ for all t also ensures tractability. Instead of equation (3.9.19) we then obtain

$$(3.9.31)\quad F_K(K_{T-1}^{c} + K_{T-1}^{w\,*}) = (1+i_{T-1})/(1-a_T^w) .$$

Inserting the optimal policy (3.9.17) into the recurrence relation from stage T-1, for $u_{T-1}=1$ we have

$$(3.9.32)\quad \begin{aligned} \Phi_{T-1} = {} & F(K_{T-2}^{c} + K_{T-2}^{w}, L_{T-2}, T-1) + (1-m_{T-1})(K_{T-2}^{c} + K_{T-2}^{w}) - \\ & F_{K,T}^{-1}\left(\frac{1+i_{T-1}}{1-a_T^w}\right) + \frac{1-a_T^w}{1+i_{T-1}}\, F\left(F_{K,T}^{-1}\left(\frac{1+i_{T-1}}{1-a_T^w}\right), L_{T-1}, T\right) \end{aligned}$$

Instead of equation (3.9.22) we obtain for $u_{T-1}=u_{T-2}=1$

$$(3.9.33)\quad F_K(K_{T-2}^{c} + K_{T-2}^{w\,*}, L_{T-2}, T-1) = i_{t-2} + m_{T-1} ,$$

which, again, is independent of the preceding capital stocks. Thus the recurrence relation on stage T-2 is computed to be

$$(3.9.34)\quad \begin{aligned} \Phi_{T-2} = {} & F(K_{T-3}^{c} + K_{T-3}^{w}, L_{T-3}, T-2) + (1-m_{T-2})(K_{T-3}^{c} + K_{T-3}^{w}) - \\ & F_{K,T-1}^{-1}(i_{T-2} + m_{T-1}) + (1+i_{T-2})^{-1}\, \Phi_{T-1}, \end{aligned}$$

where Φ_{T-1} from formula (3.9.32) only depends on

$$K_{T-2}^{c} + K_{T-2}^{w\,*} = F_{K,T-1}^{-1}(i_{T-2} + m_{T-1})$$

and

$$K_{T-1}^{c} + K_{T-1}^{w\,*} = F_{K,T}^{-1}\left(\frac{1+i_{T-1}}{1-a_T^w}\right) ,$$

too. Proceeding further in backward dynamic programming, one can show by induction after considerable computational effort

$$(3.9.35)\quad F_K(K_{t-1}^{c} + K_{t-1}^{w\,*}, L_{t-1}, t) = i_{t-1} + m_t , \qquad t = 2,..,T-1.$$

That is to say, for $u_t=1$ for all $t \leqq T-1$, we have obtained the same optimality conditions as in the cooperative case (Section 3.1) and in the case with exogeneous dividends of workers controlling wages (Section 3.2) for $u_t = 1$. We have thus derived the following

3.9.36 Theorem

Let the assumptions (A 9.1) through (A 9.6) and $u_t=1$ for all $t < T$ be satisfied for problem (P3.9). If there exists a feasible sequence of workers' capital stocks $\{K_t^{w*}\}_{t=0,..,T}$ satisfying the equations

$$(3.9.37)\quad F_K(K_{t-1}^c+K_{t-1}^w,L_{t-1},t) = i_{t-1} + m_t \quad , \qquad t=2,..,T-1$$

and

$$(3.9.38)\quad F_K(K_{T-1}^c+K_{T-1}^w,L_{T-1},T) = (1+i_{T-1})/(1-a_T^w) \qquad t=T,$$

then $\{K_t^{w*}\}_{t=0,..,T}$ constitutes a sequence of optimal capital stocks for problem (P3.9). The sequence of optimal wages $\{w_t^*\}_{t=0,..,T-1}$ is given by formula (3.9.30), too.

3.9.39 Remark

Theorem 3.9.27 and 3.9.36 contain optimal policies only for the two cases considered:

(i) $a_t^w = a_t^d = a_t$ for all t is rather unrestrictive because all it states is that in each period t, workers' saving and investment from both sources of income are the same. Both together may be different in different periods.

(ii) The assumption $u_t = 1$ for all $t < T$, on the other hand, is quite restrictive. It states that capitalists are investing agents only with zero consumption. Then the sequences of optimal capital stocks are the same as when workers control wages obtaining exogeneous dividends. Furthermore, the optimal capital stocks are identical to those from the cooperative case investigated in Section 3.1 .

Notice, it suffices for tractability that one of the above cases holds. If neither of them is given, however, then only the optimality conditions (3.9.16) and (3.9.17.) are valid. Generally for $t < T-1$, the formulas obtained are much too complicated as to be of practical or theoretical use. For special functions and parameters, however, by some computer programming results can still be obtained.

As we have seen, by becoming more realistic in allowing dividends to be endogeneous, some further restrictive assumption (which some may call unrealistic) was necessary to guarantee tractability.

3.9.2 WORKERS CONTROLLING WAGES IN THE STATE MODEL WHEN DIVIDENDS ARE ENDOGENEOUS

In this paragraph, we will allow for endogeneous dividends in the state model presented in Section 3.8. The assumptions are therefore modified as follows.

(A 9.1) *Production*

The economy's GNP in period t is given by

$$(3.9.40)\quad Y_t = F(K^c_{t-1}+K^s_{t-1}+K^w_{t-1}, L_{t-1}, t) \quad , \quad t=1,..,T,$$

where K^c_{t-1}, K^s_{t-1}, and K^w_{t-1} denote the capitalists', the state's, and the workers' capital stock shares, respectively. The production function has the same properties and depreciation is the same as was required in assumption (A 9.1).

(A 9.2') *Distribution*

Assumption (A 9.2) still applies here. Wages (3.9.2) and residuals (3.9.3) through (3.9.5) are before tax values, however.

(A 9.3') = (A 3') from page 87 .

(A 9.4') = (A 9.4) = (A 4)

(A 9.5') *Boundary Condition*

In period $t=0$, capitalists, state, and workers start up with capital stocks K_0^c, K_0^s, and $K_0^w > 0$, respectively.

(A 9.6') = (A 9.6),

where workers net income after saving and tax is now given by

$$N_t^w = (1-a_t)(1-\tau_t^w)\, w_{t-1}L_{t-1} + \frac{K_{t-1}^w}{K_{t-1}^c + K_{t-1}^w} \cdot [F(K_{t-1}^c + K_{t-1}^s + K_{t-1}^w, L_{t-1}, t) - w_{t-1}L_{t-1}],\ t=1,..,T. \tag{3.9.41}$$

Notice, by assumption (A 9.2') and (A 9.3') it is assumed that the state does not receive direct capital income from its capital stocks K_t, $t=0,..,T$. All the state receives is taxes from workers and capitalists. These and state's investment are specified in assumption (A 6) from page 86 . Thus we add to our assumptions (A 9.7') = (A 6).

Now the workers' problem is:

$$\text{Maximize} \sum_{t=1}^{T} [(1-a_t)(1-\tau_t^w)(w_{t-1}L_{t-1} + \frac{K_{t-1}^w}{K_{t-1}^c + K_{t-1}^w} \cdot [F(K_{t-1}^c + K_{t-1}^s + K_{t-1}^w, L_{t-1}, t) - w_{t-1}L_{t-1}]] \prod_{j=0}^{t-1} (1+i_j)^{-1}$$

subject to

$$\text{(P3.9')} \quad \begin{aligned} K_t^c &= u_t(1-\tau_t^c)\frac{K_{t-1}^c}{K_{t-1}^c + K_{t-1}^w} R_t + (1-m_t)K_{t-1}^c \ , \\ & \qquad\qquad\qquad\qquad\qquad\qquad t=1,..,T, \\ K_t^w &= a_t(1-\tau_t^w)(w_{t-1}L_{t-1} + \frac{K_{t-1}^w}{K_{t-1}^c + K_{t-1}^w} \cdot R_t) + (1-m_t)K_{t-1}^w \ , \end{aligned}$$

$$K_t^S = s_t^W \tau_t^W \left(w_{t-1}L_{t-1} + \frac{K_{t-1}^W}{K_{t-1}^C + K_{t-1}^W} R_t\right) + (1-m_t)K_{t-1}^S$$

(P3.9') $$+ s_t^C \tau_t^C \frac{K_{t-1}^C}{K_{t-1}^C + K_{t-1}^W} R_t \quad ,$$

where $t=1,..,T$

$$R_t = F(K_{t-1}^C + K_{t-1}^S + K_{t-1}^W, L_{t-1}, t) - w_{t-1}L_{t-1} \; ,$$

and

K_o^C, $K_o^S, K_o^W > 0$ specified.

Problem (P3.9') is trivial if $u_t + (s_t^C - u_t)\tau_t^C \leqq a_t + (s_t^W - a_t)\tau_t^W$. Thus it will be required in the remainder that for all t $u_t + (s_t^C - u_t)\tau_t^C > a_t + (s_t^W - a_t)\tau_t^W$.

The problem will also be attacked via backward dynamic programming, where $\phi_t := \phi_t(K_{t-1}^C, K_{t-1}^S, K_{t-1}^W)$ denotes the recurrence relation on stage t, $t = 1,..,T$.

$$\phi_T = \underset{w_{T-1}}{\mathrm{Max}} \left\{ (1-a_T)(1-\tau_T^W)\left[w_{T-1}L_{T-1} + \frac{K_{T-1}^W}{K_{T-1}^C + K_{T-1}^W} \cdot \right.\right.$$
$$\left.\left.(F(K_{T-1}^C + K_{T-1}^S + K_{T-1}^W, L_{T-1}, T) - w_{t-1}L_{T-1})\right]\right\} .$$

Because of

(3.9.43) $K_{t-1}^W/(K_{t-1}^C + K_{t-1}^W) < 1$ $\qquad t=1,..,T,$

the optimal control is given by

(3.9.44) $w_{T-1}^*(K_{T-1}^C, K_{T-1}^S, K_{T-1}^W) = F(K_{T-1}^C + K_{T-1}^S + K_{T-1}^W)/L_{T-1}$.

Hence

(3.9.45) $\phi_T = (1-a_T)(1-\tau_T^W)F(K_{T-1}^C + K_{T-1}^S + K_{T-1}^W, L_{T-1}, T)$,

which may be expressed as a function of $K_{T-2}^C, K_{T-2}^S, K_{T-2}^W$ and w_{T-2} by noting that, in general, for $t = 1,..,T$

$$K_t^c+K_t^s+K_t^w = [a_t+(s_t^w-a_t)\tau_t^w][w_{t-1}L_{t-1} + \frac{K_{t-1}^w}{K_{t-1}^c+K_{t-1}^w} R_t]+$$

(3.9.46)

$$[u_t+(s_t^c-u_t)\tau_t^c]\frac{K_{t-1}^c}{K_{t-1}^c+K_{t-1}^w} R_t+(1-m_t)(K_{t-1}^c+K_{t-1}^s+K_{t-1}^w),$$

where, again,

(3.9.47) $$R_t = F(K_{t-1}^c+K_{t-1}^s+K_{t-1}^w, L_{t-1}, t) - w_{t-1}L_{t-1}, \quad t=1,..,T.$$

Thus, on stage T-1, we have

$$\Phi_{T-1} = \underset{w_{T-2}}{\text{Max}} \{(1-a_{T-1})(1-\tau_{T-1}^w)\; w_{T-2}L_{T-2}+ \frac{K_{T-2}^w}{K_{T-2}^c+K_{T-2}^w}$$

(3.9.48)

$$(F(K_{T-2}^c+K_{T-2}^s+K_{T-2}^w, L_{T-2}, T-1)-w_{T-2}L_{T-2}) + (1+i_{T-1})^{-1}\Phi_T\}$$

Differentiation with respect to w_{T-2} yields as a first order condition for optimality

$$F_K(K_{T-1}^c+K_{T-1}^s+K_{T-1}^{w\;1)}, L_{T-1}, T) =$$

(3.9.49)

$$\frac{(1-a_{T-1})(1-\tau_{T-1}^w)(1+i_{T-1})}{(1-a_T)(1-\tau_T^w)\; u_{T-1}+(s_{T-1}^c-u_{T-1})\tau_{T-1}^c-a_{T-1}-(s_{T-1}^w-a_{T-1})\tau_{T-1}^w}$$

Due to concavity, this and the following conditions are sufficient for optimality. By using formula (3.9.46) the control function w_{T-2}^* can be determined. We observe that the sum $K_{T-1}^c+K_{T-1}^s+K_{T-1}^{w*}$ does not depend on the other capital stocks. By insertion of w_{T-2}^* into Φ_{T-1}, we obtain:

$$\Phi_{T-1} = \frac{(1-a_{T-1})(1-\tau_{T-1}^w)\; F(K_{T-2}^c+K_{T-2}^s+K_{T-2}^w, L_{T-2}, T-1)\; u_{T-1}+(s_{T-1}^c-}{u_{T-1} + (s_{T-1}^c - u_{T-1})\tau_{T-1}^c \quad -}$$

(3.9.50)

$$\frac{u_{T-1})\tau_{T-1}^c + (1-m_{T-1})(K_{T-2}^c+K_{T-2}^s+K_{T-2}^w)-(K_{T-1}^c+K_{T-1}^s+K_{T-1}^{w*})^{\;1)}}{- a_{T-1} - (s_{T-1}^w - a_{T-1})\tau_{T-1}^w} +$$

$$(1-a_T)(1-\tau_T^w)F(K_{T-1}^c+K_{T-1}^s+K_{T-1}^{w*\,2)}, L_{T-1}, T)/(1+i_{T-1}) \quad .$$

---

1) The sum $K_{T-1}^c+K_{T-1}^s+K_{T-1}^{w*}$ is via formula (3.9.46) a function of w_{T-2} and K_{T-2}^i.

2) Notice, these sums do not depend on the other capital stocks.

Since the recurrence relation on stage T-2 is given by

$$\Phi_{T-2} = \underset{w_{T-3}}{\mathrm{Max}} \{(1-a_{T-2})(1-\tau^{w}_{T-2})\, w_{T-3}L_{T-3} + \frac{K^{w}_{T-3}}{K^{c}_{T-3}+K^{w}_{T-3}} \cdot \tag{3.9.51}$$

$$(F(K^{c}_{T-3}+K^{s}_{T-3}+K^{w}_{T-3}, L_{T-3}, L_{T-3}, T-2) - w_{T-3}L_{-3}) + (1+i_{T-2})\Phi_{T-1}\},$$

we obtain as an optimality condition

$$F_K(K^{c}_{T-2}+K^{s}_{T-2}+K^{w\,*}_{T-2}{}^{1)}, L_{T-2}, T-1) = [\frac{1-a_{T-2}}{1-a_{T-1}} \frac{1-\tau^{w}_{T-2}}{1-\tau^{w}_{T-1}} (1+i_{T-2}) \cdot$$

$$\frac{u_{T-1}+(s^{c}_{T-1}-u_{T-1})\tau^{c}_{T-1}-a_{T-1}-(s^{w}_{T-1}-a_{T-1})\tau^{w}_{T-1}}{u_{T-2}-(s^{c}_{T-2}-u_{T-2})\tau^{c}_{T-2}-a_{T-2}-(s^{w}_{T-2}-a_{T-2})\tau^{w}_{T-2}} + m_t - 1\;]\,/ \tag{3.9.52}$$

$$[u_{T-1}+(s^{c}_{T-1}-u_{T-1})\tau^{c}_{T-1}] \quad .$$

By determining w^{*}_{T-3} we notice that, again, the sum $K^{c}_{T-2}+K^{s}_{T-2}+K^{w\,*}_{T-2}$ does not depend on the other capital stocks.

After quite some computational effort it can be shown by further dynamic programming and induction that the following optimality condition holds for all $t=1,..,T-2$.

$$F_K(K^{c}_{t}+K^{s}_{t}+K^{w}_{t}{}^{2)}, L_t, t+1) = [\frac{1-a_t}{1-a_{t+1}} \frac{1-\tau^{w}_{t}}{1-\tau^{w}_{t+1}} (1+i_t) \cdot \tag{3.9.53}$$

$$\frac{u_{t+1}+(s^{c}_{t+1}-u_{t+1})\tau^{c}_{t+1}-a_{t+1}-(s^{w}_{t+1}-a_{t+1})\tau^{w}_{t+1}}{u_t-(s^{c}_{t}-u_t)\tau^{c}_{t}-a_t-(s^{w}_{t}-a_t)\tau^{w}_{t}} + m_{t+1}-1]/[u_{t+1}+(s^{c}_{t+1}-u_{t+1})\tau^{c}_{t+1}]$$

$$t=1,..,T-2.$$

Notice, if all saving, investment, and tax parameters are constant in time, then condition (3.9.53) reduces to

---

1) Again, this sum is actually a function of w_{T-3} and K^{i}_{T-3}, $i=c,s,w$.

2) By formula (3.9.46), this sum is a function of w_{t-1} and K^{i}_{t-1}, $i=c,s,w$.

$$(3.9.54)\quad F_K(K_t^c+K_t^s+K_t^w, L_t, t+1) = \frac{i_t + m_{t+1}}{u + (s^c-u)\tau^c} \quad , \qquad t=1,..,T-2,$$

which checks with the corresponding condition (3.8.16) from Section 3.8. We have thus derived the following theorem.

3.9.55 Theorem

Let the assumptions (A 9.1') through (A 9.7') and the inequality $u_t + (s_t^c-u_t)\tau_t^c > a_t + (s_t^w-a_t)\tau_t^w$ for all t hold for problem (P3.9'). If there exists a feasible sequence of workers' capital stocks $\{K_t^{w*}\}_{t=0,..,T}$ satisfying the equations

$$(3.9.56)\quad \begin{aligned} F_K(K_{t-1}^c+K_{t-1}^s+K_{t-1}^w, L_{t-1}, t) = [\frac{1-a_{t-1}}{1-a_t}\,\frac{1-\tau_{t-1}^w}{1-\tau_t^w}\,(1+i_{t-1})\cdot \\ \frac{u_t + (s_t^c-u_t)\tau_t^c - a_t - (s_t^w-a_t)\tau_t^w}{u_{t-1}+(s_{t-1}^c-u_{t-1})\tau_{t-1}^c-a_{t-1}-(s_{t-1}^w-a_{T-1})\tau_{t-1}^w} + m_t - 1]/[u_t+(s_t^c-u_t)\tau_t^c] \end{aligned}$$

for t=2,..,T-1 and

$$(3.9.57)\quad \begin{aligned} F_K(K_{t-1}^c+K_{t-1}^s+K_{t-1}^w, L_{t-1}, t) = [\frac{1-a_{t-1}}{1-a_t}\,\frac{1-\tau_{t-1}^w}{1-\tau_t^w}\,(1+i_{t-1})]/ \\ [u_{t-1}+(s_{t-1}^c-u_{t-1})\tau_{t-1}^c-a_{t-1}-(s_{t-1}^w-a_{t-1})\tau_{t-1}^w] \end{aligned}$$

for t=T, then $\{K_t^{w*}\}_{t=0,..,T}$ constitutes a sequence of optimal workers' capital stocks for problem (P3.9'). The sequence of optimal wages $\{w_t^*\}_{t=0,..,T-1}$ can be calculated from equations (3.9.46) by inserting the optimal capital stocks satisfying the conditions above.

3.9.58 Remarks

In Theorem 3.9.55 no special requirements were necessary because, by assumption (A 9.3') = (A 3'), we have required $a_t^w = a_t^d = a_t$ for all t in all of Paragraph 3.9.2 . Thus, Theorem 3.9.55 is actually a generalization of Theorem 3.9.27.

This can be easily veryfied by letting $s_t^w=s_t^c=\tau_t^w=\tau_t^c=0$ in Theorem 3.9.55. By letting $u_t=s_t^w=s_t^c=1$ for all $t < T$, equations (3.9.56) reduce to

$$(3.9.59)\quad F_K(K_{t-1}^c+K_{t-1}^s+K_{t-1}^w, L_{t-1}, t) = i_{t-1} + m_t \quad , \qquad t=2,..,T-1,$$

and equation(3.9.57) reduces to

$$(3.9.60)\quad F_K(K_{t-1}^c+K_{t-1}^s+K_{t-1}^w, L_{t-1}, t) = \frac{1 + i_{t-1}}{(1-a_t)(1-\tau_t^w)} \quad , \; t=T.$$

Equations (3.9.59) are identical to (3.9.37) from Theorem (3.9.36). For $(1-a_T)(1-\tau_t^w) = 1-a_t^w$ equations (3.9.60) and (3.9.37) are identical, too.

It has been shown in Theorems 3.9.27 and 3.9.55 that it is possible to allow for endogeneous dividends if one is willing to require $a_t^w=a_t^d=a_t$ for all t. Under this additional condition, problems (P3.9) and (P3.9') can also be solved by a proper formulation of Theorem 6.1. It is also possible to maximize utility instead of present values and still solve the corresponding problems. However, we do not want to go into details here.

There is still another way to derive Section 3.9's theorems. One can solve equation (3.9.10) or (3.9.46) for w_{t-1} and insert the result into the objective function. For $u_t = 1$ or $a_t^w = a_t^d$ the objective functions are then additively separable with respect to $K_1^w,..,K_T^w$. By maximizing with respect to $K_1^w, K_2^w,..,K_T^w$ the optimality conditions of Theorems 3.9.27, 3.9.36, and 3.9.55 are then readily obtained.

3.10 SUMMARY

The purpose of this section is to sum up some key results of the preceding nine sections. In Chapter 4 it will then be shown how these results can be modified under somewhat different assumptions regarding the objective functions. And finally in Chapter 5 the economic relevance of all these results will be discussed.

Table 3.10.1 shows the marginal productivities of the capital stocks required in the optimality conditions when different utilities are maximized.

Objective to be maximized	$F_K(K_{t-1}, L_{t-1}, t)$, $t = 2, .., T$.	Control variable
$U^C(C_1, .., C_T)$ C_t - total consumption	$\left(\frac{\partial U^C}{\partial C_{t-1}} \middle/ \frac{\partial U^C}{\partial C_t}\right) + m_t - 1$	α_t
$U^W(W_1, .., W_T)$ W_t - total wages	$\frac{1}{u_t}\left[\frac{u_t - a_t^w}{u_{t-1} - a_{t-1}^w}\left(\frac{\partial U^W}{\partial W_{t-1}} \middle/ \frac{\partial U^W}{\partial W_t}\right) + m_t - 1\right]$	w_t
$U^R(R_1^c, .., R_T^c)$ R_t^c - capitalists' total consumption	$\left(\frac{\partial U^R}{\partial R_{t-1}^c} \middle/ \frac{\partial U^R}{\partial R_t^c}\right) + m_t - 1$	u_t
$U^N(N_1^w, .., N_T^w)$ N_t^w - workers' total consumption	$\frac{1}{u_t}\left[\left(\frac{\partial U^N}{\partial N_{t-1}^w} \middle/ \frac{\partial U^N}{\partial N_t^w}\right) + m_t - 1\right]$	a_t^w, a_t^d

Table 3.10.1

In Section 3.8, when the state was taken into account, we obtained for the utility function $U^W(W_1^n, .., W_T^n)$ (control w_t):

$$F_K(K_{t-1},L_{t-1},t) = [u_t+(s_t^c-u_t)\tau_t^c]^{-1}\cdot\left\{\left(\frac{\partial U^w}{\partial w_{t-1}^n}\Big/\frac{\partial U^w}{\partial w_t^n}\right)\frac{1-\tau_{t-1}^w}{1-\tau_t^w}\cdot\right.$$

$$\left.\frac{u_t - a_t + (s_t^c - u_t)\tau_t^c - (s_t^w - a_t)\tau_t^w}{u_{t-1}-a_{t-1}+(s_{t-1}^c-u_{t-1})\tau_{t-1}^c-(s_{t-1}^w-a_{t-1})\tau_{t-1}^w} + m_t - 1\right\},\quad t=2,..,T.$$

For capitalists' utility function $U^A(R_1^A,..,R_T^A)$ (control u_t) we obtained

$$F_K(K_{t-1},L_{t-1},t) = \frac{\left(\dfrac{\partial U^A}{\partial R_{t-1}^A}\Big/\dfrac{\partial U^A}{\partial R_t^A}\right) + m_t - 1}{1 - \tau_t^c(1 - s_t^c)}\quad ,\quad t = 2,..,T\ .$$

When we maximize the present values instead of utilities, then the time preference rate i_t, $t=0,..,T-1$, enters the results and the ratios of marginal utlities drop as the following table indicates:

Criterion in period t	$F_K(K_{t-1},L_{t-1},t)$, $t = 2,..,T$.	Control variable
C_t	$i_{t-1} + m_t$	α_t
W_t	$\frac{1}{u_t}\left[\frac{u_t - a_t^w}{u_{t-1}-a_{t-1}^w}(1+i_{t-1}) + m_t - 1\right]$	w_t
R_t^C	$i_{t-1} + m_t$	u_t
N_t^w	$\frac{1}{u_t}(i_{t-1} + m_t)$	a_t^w, a_t^d
w_t^n state	$\left\{\frac{1-\tau_{t-1}^w}{1-\tau_t^w}\,\frac{u_t- a_t + (s_t^c - u_t)\tau_t^c - (s_t^w - a_t)\tau_t^w}{u_{t-1}-a_{t-1}+(s_{t-1}^c-u_{t-1})\tau_{t-1}^c-(s_{t-1}^w-a_{t-1})\tau_{t-1}^w}\cdot(1+i_{t-1}) + m_t - 1\right\}/[u_t+(s_t^c-u_t)\tau_t^c]$.	w_t

Criterion in period t	$F_K(K_{t-1},L_{t-1},t)$, t = 2,..,T .	Control variable
R^A_t state	$(i_{t-1}+m_t)/(1-\tau^C_t(1-s^C_t))$	u_t
N^W_t endogeneous dividends	$a^W_t=a^d_t=a_t:\ \frac{1}{u_t}\left[\frac{1-a_{t-1}}{1-a_t}\frac{u_t-a_t}{u_{t-1}-a_{t-1}}(1+i_{t-1})+m_t-1\right]$ $u_t = 1\ :\ i_{t-1}+m_t$	w_t
N^W_t end. divid. state $a^W_t=a^d_t=a_t$	$\{\frac{1-a_{t-1}}{1-a_t}\,\frac{1-\tau^W_{t-1}}{1-\tau^W_t}\,\frac{u_t-a_t+(s^C_t-u_t)\tau^C_t-(s^W_t-a_t)\tau^W_t}{u_{t-1}-a_{t-1}+(s^C_{t-1}-u_{t-1})\tau^C_{t-1}-(s^W_{t-1}-a_{t-1})\tau^C_{t-1}}\cdot(1+i_{t-1})+m_t-1\}/\{u_t+(s^C_t-u_t)\tau^C_t\}$.	w_t

Table 3.10.2

It is left to the reader to check how the marginal productivities from Table 3.10.2 are simplified if the saving and investment parameters are constant in time. If all functions and parameters are constant in time, then quite nice expressions for the investment ratio and workers' share can be obtained as the following table indicates.

Criterion in period t	$\alpha_t=\alpha$, t=2,..,T-1	$\gamma_t=\gamma$, t=2,..,T-1
C_t	$\eta(k^*)(1+m)/(i+m)$	not considered in coop. case
W_t	$u\eta(k^*)(1+m)/(i+m)$	$\frac{u}{u-a}[1-\eta(k^*)(1+m)/(i+m)]$
R^C_t	$\eta(k^*)(1+m)/(i+m)$	$\frac{1}{u-a}[1-\eta(k^*)(1+m)/(i+m)]$
N^W_t	$u\eta(k^*)(1+m)/(i+m)$	$\frac{u}{u-a}[1-\eta(k^*)(1+m)/(i+m)]$
W^n_t state	$\frac{[u+(s^C-u)\tau^C]\eta(k^*)(1+m)}{i+m}$	$\frac{1-\eta(k^*)(1+m)/(i+m)}{1-[a+(s^W-a)\tau^W]/[u+(s^C-u)\tau^C]}$
N^W_t-state	$\frac{(1-\tau^C+\tau^C s^C)\eta(k^*)(1+m)}{i+m}$	$\frac{1-\eta(k^*)(1+m)(1-\tau^C+\tau^C s^C)/(i+m)(u-u\tau^C+\tau^C s^C)}{1-[a+(s^W-a)\tau^W]/[u+(s^C-u)\tau^C]}$

Table 3.10.3

4. MODIFICATIONS OF THE MODEL OF DISTRIBUTION AND WEALTH

In Sections 3.1 through 3.9 of the preceding chapter, we stated objectives to be maximized without discussing them in detail. These objectives were utility from total consumtion, total wages, total consumable residual, e.t.c... . If population and labor may change from period to period, however, it makes sense to consider per capita values instead of the aggregate values used so far.

4.1 THE COOPERATIVE CASE

For instance in Section 3.1, where the cooperative case was investigated, we also could have considered criteria depending on average consumption per worker or per capita of population. We do not wish to investigate all these alternative objectives in the same detailed way as was done in Chapter 3. It will be shown in the next tables, however, how some key results are changed under consideration of different objectives. Table 4.1 shows some alternative objectives for the cooperative case and the optimal marginal productivity of capital.

Objective to be maximized	$F_K(K_{t-1},L_{t-1},t)$, $t=2,..,T$	Control variable
$U^C(C_1,..,C_T)$ C_t - total consumption	$\left(\frac{\partial U^C}{\partial C_{t-1}} \Big/ \frac{\partial U^C}{\partial C_t}\right) + m_t - 1$	α_t
$U^c(c_1^L,..,c_T^L)$ [1] $c_t^L = C_t/L_t$	$\left(\frac{\partial U^c}{\partial c_{t-1}^L} \Big/ \frac{\partial U^c}{\partial c_t^L}\right)(1+l_t) + m_t - 1$	α_t
$U^c(c_1^N,..,c_T^N)$ $c_t^N = C_t/N_t$	$\left(\frac{\partial U^c}{\partial c_{t-1}^N} \Big/ \frac{\partial U^c}{\partial c_t^N}\right)(1+n_t) + m_t - 1$	α_t

Table 4.1

[1] This case is investigated in Buhl [1984].

If instead of utility the present values are maximized, we have to substitute $(1+i_{t-1})$ for the ratios of marginal utilities in Table 4.1 . If all functions and parameters are constant in time, then the optimal investment ratios with respect to the objectives above are given by

$$\alpha^* = \eta(k^*)(1+m)/(i+m),$$

$$\alpha_L^* = \eta(k^*)(1+m)/(i+il+l+m), \qquad t=2,..,T-1,$$

$$\alpha_N^* = \eta(k^*)(1+m)/(i+in+n+m),$$

respectively.

4.2 WHEN WORKERS CONTROL WAGES

As has become clear above, the only difference between maximization of utility or the corresponding present value in the optimality conditions is, that instead of the ratios of marginal utilities the term $(1+i_{t-1})$ appears. Thus in the following Table 4.2 we sum up some optimality conditions for maximizing present values of workers' wage incomes or total incomes. It is left to the reader to imagine the corresponding conditions for maximization of utility.

Criterion in period t	$F_K(K_{t-1},L_{t-1},t)$, $t=2,..,T$	Control variable
w_{t-1}	$\frac{1}{u_t}\left[\frac{u_t - a_t^w}{u_{t-1}-a_{t-1}^w}(1+i_{t-1})(1+l_{t-1})+m_t-1\right]$	w_t
$w_{t-1}L_{t-1}$	$\frac{1}{u_t}\left[\frac{u_t - a_t^w}{u_{t-1}-a_{t-1}^w}(1+i_{t-1}) + m_t - 1\right]$	w_t
$w_{t-1}L_{t-1}/N_{t-1}$	$\frac{1}{u_t}\left[\frac{u_t - a_t^w}{u_{t-1}-a_{t-1}^w}(1+i_{t-1})(1+n_t)+m_t - 1\right]$	w_t

Criterion in period t	$F_K(K_{t-1},L_{t-1},t),\ t=2,..,T$	Control variable
$w_{t-1}(1-a_t^w)+$ $d_{t-1}(1-a_t^d)$	$\frac{1}{u_t}\left[\frac{u_t-a_t^w}{u_{t-1}-a_{t-1}^w}\ \frac{1-a_{t-1}^w}{1-a_t^w}(1+i_{t-1})(1+l_{t-1})+m_t-1\right]$	w_t
$[w_{t-1}(1-a_t^w)+$ $d_{t-1}(1-a_t^d)]L_{t-1}$	$\frac{1}{u_t}\left[\frac{u_t-a_t^w}{u_{t-1}-a_{t-1}^w}\ \frac{1-a_{t-1}^w}{1-a_t^w}(1+i_{t-1})+m_t-1\right]$	w_t
$[w_{t-1}(1-a_t^w)+$ $d_{t-1}(1-a_t^d)]L_{t-1}/N_{t-1}$	$\frac{1}{u_t}\left[\frac{u_t-a_t^w}{u_{t-1}-a_{t-1}^w}\ \frac{1-a_{t-1}^w}{1-a_t^w}(1+i_{t-1})(1+n_t)+m_t-1\right]$	w_t

In the model with endogeneous dividends the same optimality conditions as above are obtained for $a_t^w = a_t^d$, $t = 1,..,T$.

Table 4.2

In the same way as indicated in Table 4.2, the results from the state models can be modified to account for maximization of per capita values.

If all functions and parameters are constant in time and $a_t^w = a_t^d$, then we obtain for criteria 1 and 4 from Table 4.2

$$\alpha = u\eta(k^*)(l+m)/(i+l+il+m),$$

and

$$\gamma = \frac{u}{u-a}[1-\eta(k^*)(l+m)/i+l+il+m)],$$

for $t = 2,..,T-1$.

Similarly, for criteria 2 and 5, we have

$$\alpha = u\eta(k^*)(l+m)/(i+m)$$

and

$$\gamma = \frac{u}{u-a}[1 - \eta(k^*)(l+m)/(i+m)] \ .$$

To obtain the values for the criteria 3 and 6, we only have to substitute n for l in the denominators of α and γ for criteria 1 and 4.

Finally, in this section the question will be investigated which of the criteria from Table 4.2 imply the smallest, medium, and largest capital stocks per worker for different parameter situations. The following Table 4.3 answers this question. Again, it is assumed $a_t^w = a_t^d$ for all t.

Parameter situation	Criterion implying largest k_t^*	medium k_t^*	smallest k_t^*
$0<l_t<n_{t+1}$	2,5	1,4	3,6
$l_t<0<n_{t+1}$	1,4	2,5	3,6
$l_t<n_{t+1}<0$	1,4	3,6	2,5
$0<n_{t+1}<l_t$	2,5	3,6	1,4
$n_{t+1}<0<l_t$	3,6	2,5	1,4
$n_{t+1}<l_t<0$	3,6	1,4	2,5

Table 4.3

Notice that due to the concavity of the production functions the largest marginal productivity implies the smallest capital stock per worker and the smallest marginal productivity implies the largest capital stock per worker. Notice further, in the first three situations the employment rate L_t/N_t tends to decrease while in the last three situations it tends to increase. This is exactly true if, for two consecutive periods t and t+1, we have $l_t = l_{t+1}$ and $n_t = n_{t+1}$.

To sum up the discussion above, we recall that the modifications of the objective function only imply slight modifications of the key results. We now turn to the case

4.3 WHEN CAPITALISTS CONTROL INVESTMENT

Instead of capitalists' objective from assumption (A 6.3) $U^R(R_1^C,..,R_T^C)$, where R_t^C is the total consumable residual in period t, one might also consider the corresponding per capita objective. Thus let O_t denote the number of capitalist at time t and o_t the corresponding rate of change. Let per capita consumable residual be denoted by $r_t^c = R_t^c/O_t$.

If capitalists wish to maximize their average utility from per capita consumable residual $U^r(r_1^c,..,r_T^c)$, then we obtain instead of (3.3.2) the optimality conditions

$$(4.4)\quad F_K(K_{t-1},L_{t-1},t) = \left(\frac{\partial U^r}{\partial r_{t-1}^c}\middle|\frac{\partial U^r}{\partial r_t^c}\right)(1+o_t) + m_t - 1, \qquad t=2,..,T.$$

If instead of utility the present value is maximized, we have

$$(4.5)\quad F_K(K_{t-1},L_{t-1},t) = i_{t-1} + o_t + i_{t-1}o_t + m_t\ , \qquad t=2,..,T.$$

If all functions and parameters are constant in time, then so is the capitalists' optimal investment rate and the corresponding investment ratio from period 2 through T-1. The latter is given by

$$\alpha = \eta(k^*)(1+m)/(i+o+io+m)\ .$$

Notice, if the discrete points of time are very close together, then the term 'io' is neglegibly small. Thus, in a continuous time framework, it would not show up.

4.4 WHEN WORKERS CONTROL SAVING

This case was investigated in Section 3.5. There it was stated in assumption (A 6.5) that workers wish to maximize utility from their total consumption, i.e. their total income after saving and investment. The following Table 4.4 shows alternate objectives and the corresponding optimality conditions. It does not matter there if a_t^w, a_t^d, or $a_t = a_t^w = a_t^d$ is supposed to be the control variable.

Objective to be maximized	$F_K(K_{t-1}, L_{t-1}, t)\ ,\ t = 2,..,T\ .$
$U^N(N_1^w,..,N_T^w)$ N_t^w - workers' consumption.	$\frac{1}{u_t}\left[\left(\frac{\partial U^N}{\partial N_{t-1}^w}\middle|\frac{\partial U^N}{\partial N_t^w}\right) + m_t - 1\right]$
$U^n(n_1^L,..,n_T^L)$ $n_t^L = N_t^w/L_{t-1}$	$\frac{1}{u_t}\left[\left(\frac{\partial U^n}{\partial n_{t-1}^L}\middle|\frac{\partial U^n}{\partial n_t^L}\right)(1+l_{t-1}) + m_t - 1\right]$
$U^n(n_1^N,..,n_T^N)$ $n_T^N = N_t^w/N_t$	$\frac{1}{u_t}\left[\left(\frac{\partial U^n}{\partial n_{t-1}^N}\middle|\frac{\partial U^n}{\partial n_t^N}\right)(1+n_t) + m_t - 1\right]$

Table 4.4

Again, if instead of utilities the present values are maximized, the corresponding marginal productivities are obtained from Table 4.4 by substituting $(1+i_{t-1})$ for the ratios of marginal utilities.

In the case of functions and parameters constant in time, for the three objectives from Table 4.4 the investment ratios for $t = 2,..,T-1$ are given by

$$\alpha = u\eta(k^*)(l+m)/(i+m),$$

$$\alpha = u\eta(k^*)(l+m)/(i+l+il+m),$$

and

$$\alpha = u\eta(k^*)(l+m)/(i+n+in+m),$$

respectively.

We have omitted consideration of the objectives above for both the state model and the model with endogeneous dividens. For reasons of brevity this exercise is left to the interested reader.

5. DISCUSSION OF THE RESULTS

It is the purpose of this chapter to sum up and discuss some important results from Chapters 3 and 4. Of course, all results and their implications are subject to the assumptions stated at the very beginning of Chapter 3.

As mentioned there already the cooperative case in Section 3.1 was mainly analyzed to serve as a reference solution for the implications of the group objectives investigated in the subsequent sections. It is still interesting to note that simple optimality conditions for the general case could be derived which, applied to some examples, allowed explicit calculation of optimal policies. In the case of functions and parameters constant in time (Result 3.1.26) the optimal investment ratio α^* is equal to the Golden Rule investment ratio if and only if the growth rate of population l is equal to the time preference rate i. The modifications in Section 4.1 show: If, instead of total consumption, consumption per worker is considered, then the Golden Rule result follows for a zero time preference rate. And for consumption per capita of population being considered it is sufficient that, additionally, the growth rates of population n and labor l are identical.

Comparing the optimality conditions from Section 3.2 with those from Section 3.1 we find that these coincide only under very restrictive conditions. Under some quite realistic additional conditions it follows that the same capital stocks as in the cooperative case are optimal for the workers only if capitalists invest all their residual income. Usually, when workers have full control over wages, the optimal capital stocks and the economy's production are smaller than in the cooperative case. In the case of functions and parameters constant in time the resulting investment ratio is $\alpha = u\alpha^*$, where u is capitalists' investment rate and α^* is the cooperatively optimal investment ratio. Thus, if capitalists invest 50% of their residual income, then workers' control of wages implies an investment ratio only half as large as the optimal one.

Having obtained these results, one might expect that capitalists' control of investment without consideration of social or cooperative objectives has similar implications. It is therefore surprising to find that much less restrictive conditions (3.3.5) suffice to guarantee that the same capital stocks as in the cooperative case are optimal for the capitalists. In fact, given existence of feasible capital stocks, this is generally true if maximization of present values instead of utilities is considered. For this case the same capital stocks, investment ratios, and output values are obtained in both, Sections 3.1 and 3.3. Considering the coincidence of these results and the divergence of the results from Section 3.2 outlined above, the key result from Section 3.4 comes quite natural: In a game theoretic situation with capitalists controlling investment and workers controlling wages usually rather restrictive conditions are necessary for the existence of a dual-stable Nash equilibrium. Result (3.4.10) shows that in such an equilibrium capitalists are required to invest all their residual income.

Seeking for reasons why capitalists are in such a weak position above, we observe that their control opportunities seem to be weaker than those of the workers, too. Since employment is supposed to be exogeneously specified, workers can control the total wage bill via the average wage rate. Capitalists, on the other hand, have no choice but to accept this wage bill as exogenous. Thus, in Section 3.5 we consider a weaker position for the workers. Wages are now assumed to be exogeneously specified and workers can only control their saving and investment rates. It is assumed that they seek to maximize their utility from consumption, i.e., net income after saving. Surprisingly we find again, that quite restrictive conditions are necessary for coincidence with the results from Sections 3.1 or 3.3. For maximization of present values it is again necessary that capitalists are investing agents only.

For more detail, see Remarks (3.5.11). Considering these explanations it is to be expected that the results of Section 3.6, where the non-cooperative case of capitalists controlling investment and workers controlling saving is analyzed, are very similar to those from Section 3.4.

The assumption of exogeneous employment is skipped in Section 3.7. While workers may control wages capitalists can now choose employment depending on the wage rate. Theorem (3.7.3) shows that capitalists choose employment in such a way that the marginal productivity of labor is equal to the wage rate if they maximize the utility from their consumable residual. Given workers know capitalists' employment policy, it is interesting to observe that via the wage rate workers may indirectly control employment. If they wish to maximize their utility from total wages, they need to solve T independent problems (WP_t), $t=1,..,T$. In the general case of production functions only assumed neo-classical, workers may or may not choose a full employment wage rate. For several well-known neo-classical production functions, however, it is shown in Theorem (3.7.30) that workers' optimal wage rate is always implying full employment.

While so far we have only distinguished workers and capitalists, the state is accounted for in Section 3.8. It is shown that the results of Sections 3.1 through 3.3 can be generalized accordingly. Finally in Section 3.9 workers' dividends are considered to be endogeneous. It is shown that in the general case the problem is considerably harder. If one is willing, however, to add some more condition quite similar results as in the case of exogeneous dividends can be obtained.

As mentioned earlier already, Chapter 4 contains some alternate objectives and shows how some key results from Chapter 3 are then modified. The economic implications are quite similiar to those discussed above.

Summing up the discussion above, we can state within the limits of the neo-classical framework considered: If workers have full control over either wages or their saving and investment, and capitalists are not investing agents only, then it is to be expected in the non-cooperative case that capital stocks and output are smaller than in the cooperative case. If workers may control wages and capitalists may control employment accordingly, then for a large number of production functions a full employment generating wage rate is optimal for the workers. In the general case,however, this may or may not be true.

6. MATHEMATICAL APPENDIX

6.1 DYNAMIC PROGRAMMING PROBLEMS WITH ADDITIVE CRITERIA

A general formulation of the dynamic programming problem with one-state-dependent functions is given by

$$\text{Maximize} \quad \sum_{t=1}^{T} g_t(x_{t-1},u_t)$$

subject to

$$\text{(P)} \qquad \left.\begin{aligned} x_t &= f_t(x_{t-1},u_t) \\ u_t &= \Omega_t, x_t \in \Xi_t \end{aligned}\right\} \quad (t=1,\ldots T)$$

$$x_o \in \Xi_o \quad \text{(specified)}$$

For $t=1,\ldots,T$, the *state space* Ξ_t and the *control space* Ω_t are contained in some supersets Ξ and Ω. $\Xi^+ = \prod_{t=1}^{T} \Xi_t$ is called the *global state space* and $\Omega^+ = \prod_{t=1}^{T} \Omega_t$ the *global control space*. The functions f and g are defined on $\Xi \times \Omega$ and take on values in Ξ and $\mathbb{R}$, respectively. The product sets Ξ^T and Ω^T are defined in the usual way.

A generalization of dynamic programming problems (P), frequently encountered in economic models employing the concept of utility functions is

$$\text{Maximize } U(y_1,\ldots,y_T)$$

subject to

$$\text{(UP)} \qquad \left.\begin{aligned} y_t &= g_t(x_{t-1},u_t) \\ x_t &= f_t(x_{t-1},u_t) \\ y_t &\in \mathbb{R},\ x_t \in \Xi_t,\ u_t \in \Omega_t \end{aligned}\right\} \quad (t=1,\ldots,T)$$

$$x_o \in \Xi_o \quad \text{(specified)}$$

Usually, the function $U: \mathbb{R}^T \to \mathbb{R}$ is assumed to be continuously differentiable, concave and increasing, which is to be assumed further.

In Buhl/Siedersleben [1984] we have shown that if there exist functions G_t and H_t such that

$$\text{(IA)}\quad g_t(x_{t-1},u_t) \equiv G_t(x_{t-1}) + H_t(f_t(x_{t-1},u_t)) \qquad t=1,\dots,T$$

and given certain reachability conditions precisely specified there [1], the solution(s) of problem (P) can be obtained by solving the simple unconstrained problem

$$\text{(R)}\quad \text{Maximize} \sum_{t=1}^{T} \Phi_t(x_t)$$

$$x_t \in \Xi_t,$$

where

$$\Phi_t(x_t) = \begin{cases} H_t(x_t) + G_{t+1}(x_t) & t=1,\dots,T-1 \\ H_t(x_t) & t=T \end{cases}.$$

The following theorem shows, how problem (UP) may be solved in special but relevant cases if conditions (IA) are satisfied.

<u>6.1 Theorem</u>

Let $\Xi_t \subseteq \mathbb{R}$, $\Omega_t \subseteq \mathbb{R}$, Ξ_t be convex and conditions (IA) be satisfied for all $t=1,\dots,T$.

Assume further that the functions $G_t : \Xi \to \mathbb{R}$, $H_t : \Xi \to \mathbb{R}$, and the increasing function $U : \mathbb{R}^T \to \mathbb{R}$ are concave and differentiable.

If there exists a feasible sequence $\{x_t^*\}_{t=0,1,\dots,T}$ satisfying the equation system [2]

---

1) It suffices that some sequence of optimal states $\{x_t^*\}_{t=1,\dots,T}$ obtained from problem (R) constitutes a feasible path for problem (P), i.e., there exists some sequence $\{u_t^*\}_{t=1,\dots,T}$ such that $x_t^* = f_t(x_{t-1}^*, u_t^*)$ for all t.

2) If $x_T \in \Xi_T$ is specified, then the equation for t=T vanishes.

$$\frac{\partial U}{\partial y_t} \cdot H_t'(x_t) + \frac{\partial U}{\partial y_{t+1}} \cdot G_{t+1}'(x_t) = 0^{1)} \quad , \; t=1,\ldots,T-1,$$

(OA)

$$\frac{\partial U}{\partial y_T} \cdot H_T'(x_T) = 0 \quad , \; t=T,$$

then it constitutes an optimal solution to problem (UP).

Proof

From the problem (UP)'s formulation and conditions (IA) it follows for all feasible sequences $\{x_t\}_{t=0,1,\ldots,T}$

$$U(y_1,\ldots,y_T) = U(g_1(x_o,u_1),\ldots, g_T(x_{T-1},u_T)) =$$

$$U(G_1(x_o) + H_1(x_1), G_2(x_1) + H_2(x_2),\ldots, G_T(x_{T-1}) + H_T(x_T))$$

As a necessary condition for an interior maximum one obtains [1)]

$$\frac{\partial U}{\partial x_t} = \frac{\partial U}{\partial y_t}\frac{dH_t}{dx_t} + \frac{\partial U}{\partial y_{t+1}}\frac{dG_{t+1}}{dx_t} = 0 \quad , \; t=1,\ldots,T-1 ,$$

and

$$\frac{\partial U}{\partial x_T} = \frac{\partial U}{\partial y_T}\frac{dH_T}{dx_T} = 0 \quad , \; t=T.$$

Since both G_t and H_t are concave and U is both increasing and concave with respect to all $y_1,\ldots,y_T$, U is also concave with respect to all $x_o,\ldots,x_T$. Formally this is shown for some x_t , $0 < t < T$, letting $\lambda,\mu \in [0,1]$, $\lambda + \mu = 1$. Then

$$U(..,G_t(x_{t-1})+H_t(\underbrace{\lambda x_t^1+\mu x_t^2}_{=:x_t}),G_{t+1}(\underbrace{\lambda x_t^1+\mu x_t^2}_{=:x_t})+H_{t+1}(x_{t+1}),..)$$

---

1) By this abbreviation we mean, just as previously,

$$\left.\frac{\partial U}{\partial y_t}(y_1,\ldots,y_T)\right|_{y_t = H_t(x_t) + G_t(x_{t-1}),\; t=1,\ldots,T.}$$

$$\geqq U(..,G_t(x_{t-1})+\lambda H_t(x_t^1)+\mu H_t(x_t^2),\lambda G_{t+1}(x_t^1)+\mu G_{t+1}(x_t^2)+H_{t+1}(x_{t+1}),..)$$

$$\geqq \lambda U(..,G_t(x_{t-1})+H_t(x_t^1),G_{t+1}(x_t^1)+H_{t+1}(x_{t+1}),..)$$

$$+\mu U(..,G_t(x_{t-1})+H_t(x_t^2),G_{t+1}(x_t^2)+H_{t+1}(x_{t+1}),..)$$

The first inequality follows from the concavity of G_{t+1} and H_t and the monotonicity of U, while the second inequality follows from the concavity of U with respect to all arguments noting that

$$\lambda G_t(x_{t-1}) + \mu G_t(x_{t-1}) = G_t(x_{t-1})$$

and

$$\lambda H_{t+1}(x_{t+1}) + \mu H_{t+1}(x_{t+1}) = H_{t+1}(x_{t+1}) \quad .$$

Due to the concavity of $U : \mathbb{R}^T \to \mathbb{R}$ with respect to all $x_o,\ldots,x_T$ each feasible stationary solution satisfying the first order conditions for optimality (OA) maximizes the function $U : \mathbb{R}^T \to \mathbb{R}$.

q.e.d.

6.2 Corollary

If the function $U: \mathbb{R}^T \to \mathbb{R}$ is given by

$$U(y_1,\ldots,y_T) = \sum_{t=1}^{T} U_t(y_t) \prod_{j=0}^{t-1} (1+i_j)^{-1} ,$$

where $U_t: \mathbb{R} \to \mathbb{R}$ and $i_t \in [0,\infty)$, then the preceding theorem's equation system reduces to

$$U_t'(H_t(x_t)+G_t(x_{t-1}))(1+i_t)H_t'(x_t)$$

$$+ U_{t+1}'(H_{t+1}(x_{t+1})+G_{t+1}(x_t))G_{t+1}'(x_t) = 0 \qquad t=1,\ldots,T-1$$

(O1)

$$U_T'(H_T(x_T)+G_T(x_{T-1}))H_T'(x_T) = 0 \qquad t=T$$

If we have $U_t(y_t) = y_t$, then we obtain the equation system[1)]

$$(1+i_t)H_t'(x_t)+G_{t+1}'(x_t) = 0 \qquad t=1,\dots,T-1$$
(O2)
$$H_T'(x_T) = 0 \qquad t=T\ .$$

6.2 DYNAMIC PROGRAMMING PROBLEMS WITH MULTIPLICATIVE CRITERIA AND GENERALIZATIONS

Another class of problems solvable via dynamic programming is the following

$$\text{Maximize} \prod_{t=1}^{T} g_t(x_{t-1},u_t)$$

(M) Subject to

$$\left.\begin{aligned} x_t &= f_t(x_{t-1},u_t) \\ x_t &\in \Xi_t,\ u_t \in \Omega_t \end{aligned}\right\} \qquad (t=1,\dots,T)$$

$$x_o \in \Xi_o \quad \text{(specified)}\ ,$$

Where $g_t: \Xi \times \Omega \to \mathbb{R}_t \subseteq \mathbb{R}_+$ are positive valued functions. Again, we call a sequence of states $\{x_t\}_{t=0,1,\dots,T}$ reachable, if there exists a sequence $\{u_t\}_{t=1,\dots,T}$, such that $x_t = f_t(x_{t-1},u_t)$ for all t.

Corresponding to conditions (IA) for problem (P) of the preceding chapter, we can state conditions (IM) for problem (M), which may simplify problem (M) in particular instances considerably:

There exist positive-valued functions G_t and H_t such that for all t

(IM) $$g_t(x_{t-1},u_t) \equiv G_t(x_{t-1}) \cdot H_t(f_t(x_{t-1},u_t)).$$

Now, if conditions (IM) hold, we have for all reachable sequences $\{x_t\}_{t=0,\dots,T}$:

$$\prod_{t=1}^{T} g_t(x_{t-1},u_t) \overset{(IM)}{=} \prod_{t=1}^{T} G_t(x_{t-1})H_t(f_t(x_{t-1},u_t)) \overset{(Reach.)}{=\!=\!=}$$

---

1) This special result has already been utilized in Buhl [1983], [1984], Buhl/Siedersleben [1984], and Buhl/Eichhorn [1984].

$$= \prod_{t=1}^{T} G_t(x_{t-1})H_t(x_t) = G_1(x_o)\left(\prod_{t=1}^{T-1} G_{t+1}(x_t)H_t(x_t)\right) \cdot H_T(x_T)$$

Thus, if there exists some reachable sequence of optimal states $\{x_t^*\}$ of the unconstrained problem

$$\text{(RM)} \quad \begin{aligned} &\text{Maximize } \prod_{t=1}^{T} \Phi_t(x_t) \\ &\text{subject to } x_t \in \Xi_t \quad , \end{aligned}$$

where

$$\Phi_t = \begin{cases} G_{t+1}(x_t) \cdot H_t(x_t) & t=1,\dots,T-1 \\ H_T(x_T) & t=T \quad , \end{cases}$$

then it constitutes an optimal solution to problem (M).

Since problem (RM) is as simple to solve as problem (R) from the preceding chapter, we propose to attack problems (M) (or (P)) in the following way:

(i) First, it should be checked, whether conditions (IM) hold for problem (M) (or conditions (IA) for problem (P)).

(ii) If so, one can formulate and solve problem (RM) (or (R)).

(iii) Now, if there exist some reachable sequence of optimal states of problem (RM) (or (R)), we have obtained an optimal solution to problem (M) (or (P)).

(iv) If not, we at least have obtained the information, how the optimal solution to problem (M) (or (P)) looked like, if the optimal states or all states would be reachable. Then, the optimal solution to problem (M) (or (P)) needs to be computed by standard dynamic methods.

Obviously, in case of reachability, problems (P) with condition (IA) and problems (M) with conditions (IM) can be solved quite similarly. Insight into the reason why this is the case gives the following theorem:

6.3 Theorem

If the functions g_t in problem (M) assume strictly positive values only, i.e. $g_t: \Xi \times \Omega \rightarrow \mathbb{R}_{++}$ for all t, then problems (P) with conditions (IA) are equivalent to problems (M) with conditions (IM).

Proof

Note, for strictly positive-valued functions g_t sequences $\{x_t^*\}$ and $\{u_t^*\}$ maximizing the objective function of problem (M) also maximize the objective function

$$\sum_{t=1}^{T} \ln g_t(x_{t-1},u_t)$$

From conditions (IM) it follows

$$\ln g_t(x_{t-1},u_t) \equiv \ln G_t(x_{t-1}) + \ln H_t(f_t(x_{t-1},u_t))$$

Thus, a problem (M) with conditions (IM) can easily be transformed into a problem (P) with conditions (IA). Conversely, all sequences $\{x_t^*\}$ and $\{u_t^*\}$ maximizing the objective function of problem (P) also maximize the objective function

$$\prod_{t=1}^{T} \exp g_t(x_{t-1},u_t) \ .$$

Note, that each $\tilde{g}_t(x_{t-1},u_t) := \exp g_t(x_{t-1},u_t)$ assumes strictly positive values only. From conditions (IA), we have

$$\exp g_t(x_{t-1},u_t) \equiv \exp G_t(x_{t-1}) \cdot \exp H_t(f_t(x_{t-1},u_t)) \ .$$

Thus, a problem (P) with conditions (IA) can also be transformed into a problem (M) with conditions (IM), which completes the proof.

Note, that problem (UP) not only is a generalization of problem (P), but also a generalization of problem (M). The following theorem shows, how problem (UP) may be solved in special but relevant cases if conditions (IM) hold.

6.4 Theorem

Let $\Xi_t \subseteq \mathbb{R}$, $\Omega_t \subseteq \mathbb{R}$, Ξ_t be convex and conditions (IM) be satisfied for t=1,...,T. Assume further that the functions $G_t\colon \Xi \to \mathbb{R}_+$, $H_t\colon \Xi \to \mathbb{R}_+$ and the increasing function $U\colon \mathbb{R}^T \to \mathbb{R}$ are concave and differentiable.

If there exists a feasible sequence $\{x_t^*\}_{t=0,\dots,T}$ satisfying the equation system[1)]

[1)] If $x_T \in \Xi_T$ is specified, too, the equation for t=T vanishes.

$$\text{(OM)}\quad \begin{aligned} &\frac{\partial U}{\partial y_t} \cdot H_t'(x_t)G_t(x_{t-1}) + \frac{\partial U}{\partial y_{t+1}} \cdot G_{t+1}'(x_t)H_{t+1}(x_{t+1}) = 0, \quad t=1,..,T-1,^{1)} \\ &\frac{\partial U}{\partial y_T} \cdot H_T'(x_T)G_T(x_{T-1}) = 0, \quad t=T, \end{aligned}$$

then it constitutes an optimal solution to problem (UP).

Proof

The proof of Theorem 6.4 follows closely the one for Theorem 6.1. By conditions (IM), we have for all feasible sequences

$$U(y_1,\ldots,y_T) = U(G_1(x_o)H_1(x_1), G_2(x_1)H_2(x_2),\ldots,G_T(x_{T-1})H_T(x_T))$$

As first order conditions for optimality, we obtain (OM).
$U\colon \mathbb{R}_+^T \to \mathbb{R}$ is, again, concave with respect to all x_t. To prove this let $\lambda,\mu \in [0,1]$, $\lambda+\mu = 1$:

$$U(..,G_t(x_{t-1})H_t(\underbrace{\lambda x_t^1+\mu x_t^2}_{=:x_t}),G_{t+1}(\lambda x_t^1+\mu x_t^2)H_{t+1}(x_{t+1}),..) \geqq$$

$$U(..,\lambda G_t(x_{t-1})H_t(x_t^1)+\mu G_t(x_{t-1})H_t(x_t^2), \lambda G_{t+1}(x_t^1)H_{t+1}(x_{t+1})+\mu G_{t+1}(x_t^2)H_{t+1}(x_{t+1}),..) \geqq$$

$$\lambda U(..,G_t(x_{t-1})H_t(x_t^1),G_{t+1}(x_t^1)H_{t+1}(x_{t+1}),..) + \mu U(..,G_t(x_{t-1})H_t(x_t^2),G_{t+1}(x_t^2)H_{t+1}(x_{t+1}),..)$$

Again, the first inequality follows from the concavity of H_t and G_{t+1} and the monotonicity of U, where as the second follows from the concavity of U. Thus, every stationary solution constitutes a global maximum.

Note, if the functions g_t and thus the functions G_t and H_t assume strictly positive values only, then problem (UP) with conditions (IM) can easily be transformed into a problem (UP) with conditions (IA). Then the result of Theorem 6.4 follows straight from Theorem 6.1.

---

1) Again, for simplicity of notation, the derivatives' arguments are omitted. See footnote 1) to the optimality condition of Theorem 6.1 .

6.5 Corollary

If the function $U: \mathbb{R}_+^T \to \mathbb{R}$ is given by

$$U(y_1,\dots,y_T) = \prod_{t=1}^{T} U_t(y_t) \prod_{j=0}^{t-1} (1+i_j)^{-1} \quad ,$$

where $U_t: \mathbb{R}_+ \to \mathbb{R}_+$ and $i_t \in [0,\infty)$, then the preceeding theorem's equation system reduces to

$$\begin{aligned} &U_t'(H_t(x_t)G_t(x_{t-1}))(1+i_t)H_t'(x_t)G_t(x_{t-1}) + \\ \text{(OM1)}\ &U_{t+1}'(G_{t+1}(x_t)H_{t+1}))G_{t+1}'(x_t)H_{t+1}(x_{t+1}) = 0 \end{aligned} \qquad t=1,\dots,T-1$$

$$U_T'(H_T(x_T)G_T(x_{T-1}))H_T'(x_T)G_T(x_{T-1}) = 0 \qquad t=T$$

If we have $U_t(y_t) = y_t$, we obtain

$$\text{(OM2)}\ (1+i_t)H_t'(x_t)G_t(x_{t-1}) + G_{t+1}'(x_t)H_{t+1}(x_{t+1}) = 0 \qquad t=1,\dots,T-1$$

$$H_T'(x_T)G_T(x_{T-1}) = 0 \qquad t=T \quad .$$

A generalization of conditions (IA) and (IM) are the following conditions

For all t there exists some function F_t such that

$$\text{(I)} \qquad g_t(x_{t-1},u_t) \equiv F_t(x_{t-1},f_t(x_{t-1},u_t)) \quad .$$

The following theorem generalizes and illustrates the results of Theorems 6.1 and 6.4.

6.6 Theorem

Let $\Xi_t \in \mathbb{R}$, $\Omega_t \in \mathbb{R}$, Ξ_t be convex and conditions (I) be satisfied for all t=1,...,T . Assume further that the function $F_t: \Xi_t^2 \to \mathbb{R}$ and the increasing function $U: \mathbb{R}^T \to \mathbb{R}$ are concave and differentiable.

If there exists a feasible sequence $\{x_t^*\}_{t=0,\dots,T}$ satisfying the equation system

$$
(O) \quad \begin{cases} \dfrac{\partial U}{\partial y_t} \cdot \dfrac{\partial F_t}{\partial x_t}(x_{t-1},x_t) + \dfrac{\partial U}{\partial y_{t+1}} \cdot \dfrac{\partial F_{t+1}}{\partial x_t}(x_t,x_{t+1}) = 0, & t=1,..,T-1, \\[2ex] \dfrac{\partial U}{\partial y_T} \cdot \dfrac{\partial F_T}{\partial x_T}(x_{T-1},x_T) = 0, & t=T, \text{ [1]} \end{cases}
$$

then it constitutes an optimal solution to problem (UP).

The proof of Theorem 6.6 is very similar to the ones of Theorems 6.1. and 6.4 and thus may be omitted here. Note that both conditions (OA) and conditions (OM) are special cases of conditions (O) only.

6.7 Remark

Notice, in Theorems 6.1, 6.4, and 6.6 no special assumptions about the form of U were required except that U be concave and increasing with respect to all $y_1,..,y_T$. Thus, for instance, the function U: $\mathbb{R}^T \to \mathbb{R}$ from Theorem 6.1 may have the form of the objective function in problem (M) if g_t, G_t, and H_t are positive-valued. Conversely, the function U: $\mathbb{R}^T \to \mathbb{R}$ from Theorem 6.4 may have the form of the objective function in problem (P). In either case U is increasing and concave with respect to all arguments.

[1] Again, if x_T is specified, then this equation vanishes.

7. REFERENCES

Benhabib,J./Nishimura,K.: "Competitive Equilibrium Cycles", Working Paper, New York University and University of Southern California, 1984.

Böhm-Bawerk, E.v. "Positive Theory of Capital", Vol.II of "Capital and Interest", Libertarian Press, New York, 1959, translated from forth edition, 1921.

Brems,H.: "Alternative Theories of Pricing, Distribution, Saving, and Investment", American Economic Review,69, 1979.

Bürk,R. : "Kooperation und Konflikt in einem dynamischen makroökonomischen Kreislaufmodell", Dissertation, Department of Economics, University of Karlsruhe, 1976.

Buhl,H. : "Dynamic Programming Solutions for Economic Models Requiring Little Information about the Future", in *Eichhorn,W./Henn,R.,eds.,* Mathematical Systems in Economics 86, Athenäum-Hain, Meisenheim-Königstein/Taunus, 1983 .

________*:* "A Discrete Model of Economic Growth", Journal of Macroeconomics, 1984.

________*:* "Some Environmental Aspects of Optimal Economic Growth", in *Feichtinger,G.,ed.,* Economic Application of Control Theory, North-Holland, Amsterdam, 1985.

_______*/Eichhorn,W.:* "Optimal Growth for Resource-Dependent Economies", in *Hammer,G./Pallaschke,D.,eds.,* Selected Topics in Operations Research and Mathematical Economics, Springer, Berlin, 1984.

_______*/Siedersleben,J.:* "On A Class of Dynamic Programming Problems, whose Optimal Controls Are Independent of the Future", European Journal of Operational Research, 1984.

Chakravarty, S. "Optimal Saving with Finite Planning Horizon", International Economic Review, 1962.

_______________ "Optimal Programme of Capital Accumulation in a Multi-Sector Economy", Econometrica, 1965.

_______________ "Optimal Saving with Finite Planning Horizon: A Reply", International Economic Review, 1966.

Diewert, W.: "Separability and a Generalization of the Cobb-Douglas Cost, Production, and Indirect Utility Function", Technical Report 86, Institute for Mathematical Studies in the Social Sciences, Stanford University, 1973.

__________*:* "Functional Forms for Factor and Revenue Requirement Functions", International Economic Review, 15, 1974.

Dockner, E./Feichtinger, G./Mehlmann, A.: "Non-Cooperative Solutions for a Differential Game Model of the Common Property Fishery", Working Paper 65, Institute for Econometrics and Operations Research, Technical University Vienna, Austria, 1983.

Eichhorn, W./Gleißner, W./Buhl, H.: "The Optimal Investment Ratio of an Economy with Changing Depreciation of Capital, Discounting of Future Consumption, and Exogeneous Technical Progress", in *Eichhorn, W. et.al., ed.*, Quantitative Studies on Production and Prices, Physika, Würzburg-Wien, 1982.

Feichtinger, G./Dockner, E.: "A Note on Jörgensen's Logarithmic Advertising Differential Game", Zeitschrift für Operations Research, 28, 1984.

Goldman, S.M. "Optimal Growth and Continual Planning Revision", Review of Economic Studies, 1968.

Hamada, K. "On the Optimal Transfer and Income Distribution in a Growing Economy", Review of Economic Studies, 1967.

Hammond, P.J. "Agreeable Plans with Many Capital Goods", Review of Economic Studies, 1975.

______________/*Mirrlees, J.A.* "Agreeable Plans", in *Mirrlees, J.A./Stern, N.H.* "Models of Economic Growth", Macmillan, London, 1975.

Harrod,R.: "Towards a Dynamic Economics", Macmillan, London, 1948.

Hoel,M. : "Aspects of Distribution and Growth in a Capitalist Economy", Memorandum from Institute of Economics, University of Oslo, Norway, 1975.

________*:* "Distribution and Growth as a Differential Game between Workers and Capitalists", International Economic Review, 19, 1978.

Infante, E.F./Stein, J.L. "Optimal Growth with Robust Feedback Control", Review of Economic Studies, 1973.

Kaldor,N.: "Alternative Theories of Distribution", Review of Economic Studies, 23, 1955/56.

Koopmans, T.C. "Intertemporal Distribution and 'Optimal' Aggregate Economic Growth" in *Fellner, W. et.al.*, ed., "Ten Economic Studies in the Tradition of Irving Fisher", Wiley, New York, 1967.

Krelle,W./Schunk,J./Siebke,J.:"Überbetriebliche Ertragsbeteiligung der Arbeitnehmer", Vol I,II, Tübingen, West-Germany, 1968.

_________: "Wachstum und Vermögensverteilung bei Ergebnisbeteiligung der Arbeitnehmer", in *Enke,H./Köhler,W./Schulz, W.,eds.*, Struktur und Dynamik der Wirtschaft, Haufe, Freiburg, 1983.

Lancaster,K.: "The Dynamic Inefficiency of Capitalism", Journal of Political Economy, 81, 1973.

Leitmann,G.: "Einführung in die Theorie optimaler Steuerungen und der Differentialspiele", Oldenbourg, München-Wien, 1974.

Machaczek,W.: "Mathematische Ansätze in der Verteilungstheorie", thesis, Institute for Economic Theory and Operations Research, University of Karlsruhe, West-Germany, 1984.

Majumdar,M./Nermuth,M.: "Dynamic Optimization in Non-Convex Models with Irreversible Investment: Monotonicity and Turnpike Results", Zeitschrift für Nationalökonomie, 1982.

Maneschi, A. "Optimal Saving with Finite Planning Horizon: A Note", International Economic Review, 1966a.

_____________ "Optimal Saving with Finite Planning Horizon: A Rejoinder", International Economic Review, 1966b.

Meade,J.: "A Neo-Classical Theory of Economic Growth", Unwin, London, 1964.

________: "The Outcome of the Pasinetti Process: A Note", Economic Journal, 76, 1966.

Meadows, D. et.al. "The Limits to Growth", Universe Books, New York, 1972.

Mehlmann,A./Willing,R.: "On Nonunique Closed-Loop Nash Equilibria for a Class of Differential Games with a Unique and Degenerated Feedback Solution", Journal of Optimization Theory and Applications, 41, 1983.

Mesarovic, M./Pestel, E. "Menschheit am Wendepunkt", Deutsche Verlagsanstalt, Stuttgart, 1974.

Mirrlees, J.A. "Optimum Growth when Technology is Changing", Review of Economic Studies, 1967.

Mitra,T./Ray,D.: "Dynamic Optimization on a Non-Convex Feasible Set: Some General Results for Non-Smooth Technologies", Working Paper 305, Department of Economics, Cornell University, 1983.

Neumann,K.: "Operations Research Verfahren", II, Hanser, München-Wien, 1977.

Pasinetti,L.: "Growth and Income Distribution", Cambridge University Press, 1974.

____________ "Rate of Profit and Income Distribution in Relation to the Rate of Economic Growth", Review of Economic Studies, 29, 1961/62.

Phelps,E.: "Golden Rules of Economic Growth", Norton, New York, 1966.

____________*/Pollak, R.A.* "On Second-Best National Saving and Game Equilibrium Growth", Review of Economic Studies, 1969.

Pohjola,M.: "Workers Investment Funds and the Dynamic Inefficiency of Capitalism", Journal of Public Economics, 20, 1983a.

__________: "Nash and Stackelberg Solutions in a Differential Game Model of Capitalism", Journal of Economic Dynamics and Control, 6, 1983b.

__________: "Threats and Bargaining in Capitalism", Working Paper, University of Helsinki, Finland, 1983c. (submitted to Journal of Economic Dynamics and Control)

__________: "Union Rivalry and Economic Growth", Working Paper, University of Helsinki, Finland, 1984a. (to be published in the Scandinavian Journal of Economics)

__________: "Growth, Distribution, and Employment Modelled as a Differential Game", Working Paper, University of Helsinki, Finland, 1984b.

Ramanathan,R.: "Introduction to the Theory of Economic Growth", Springer, Berlin, 1982.

Ramsey, F.P. "A Mathematical Theory of Saving", Economic Journal, 1928.

Revankar,N.: "A Class of Variable Elasticity of Substitution Production Functions", Econometrica, 39, 1971.

Ryder, H.E./Heal, G.M. "Optimal Growth with Intertemporally Dependent Preferences", Review of Economic Studies, 1973.

Samuelson,P./Modigliani,F.: "The Pasinetti Paradox in Neo-Classical and More General Models", Review of Economic Studies, 33, 1966.

Solow,R.: "A Contribution to the Theory of Economic Growth", Quarterly Journal of Economics, 1956.

________: "Technical Progress, Capital Formation, and Economic Growth", American Economic Review, 1962.

Stanley, O. "Distributional Goals and Optimal Growth", Review of Economic Studies, 1978.

Starr,H./Ho,Y.: "Nonzero-Sum Differential Games", Journal of Optimization Theory and Applications, 3, 1969.

Takayama,A.: "Mathematical Economics", Hindsdale, 1974.

Tobin,J.: "Towards a General Kaldorian Theory of Distribution", Review of Economic Studies, 27, 1963.

Vellupillai,K.: "When Workers Save and Invest: Some Kaldorian Dynamics", Zeitschrift für Nationalökonomie, 42, 1982.

Wan,H. : "Economic Growth", Harcourt Brace Jovanovich, New York, 1971.

Weizsäcker, C.C.v. "Das Investitionsoptimum in einer wachsenden Wirtschaft" in *Henn, R./Bombach, G./Böventer, E.v.* "Optimales Wachstum und Optimale Standortverteilung", Duncker und Humblot, Berlin, 1962a.

______________ "Wachstum, Zins und optimale Investitionsquote", Kyklos, Basel, 1962b.

______________ "Existence of Optimal Programs of Accumulation for an Infinite Time Horizon", Review of Economic Studies, 1965.

______________ "Lemmas for a Theory of Approximate Optimal Growth",Review of Economic Studies, 1967.

Vol. 157: Optimization and Operations Research. Proceedings 1977. Edited by R. Henn, B. Korte, and W. Oettli. VI, 270 pages. 1978.

Vol. 158: L. J. Cherene, Set Valued Dynamical Systems and Economic Flow. VIII, 83 pages. 1978.

Vol. 159: Some Aspects of the Foundations of General Equilibrium Theory: The Posthumous Papers of Peter J. Kalman. Edited by J. Green. VI, 167 pages. 1978.

Vol. 160: Integer Programming and Related Areas. A Classified Bibliography. Edited by D. Hausmann. XIV, 314 pages. 1978.

Vol. 161: M. J. Beckmann, Rank in Organizations. VIII, 164 pages. 1978.

Vol. 162: Recent Developments in Variable Structure Systems, Economics and Biology. Proceedings 1977. Edited by R. R. Mohler and A. Ruberti. VI, 326 pages. 1978.

Vol. 163: G. Fandel, Optimale Entscheidungen in Organisationen. VI, 143 Seiten. 1979.

Vol. 164: C. L. Hwang and A. S. M. Masud, Multiple Objective Decision Making – Methods and Applications. A State-of-the-Art Survey. XII, 351 pages. 1979.

Vol. 165: A. Maravall, Identification in Dynamic Shock-Error Models. VIII, 158 pages. 1979.

Vol. 166: R. Cuninghame-Green, Minimax Algebra. XI, 258 pages. 1979.

Vol. 167: M. Faber, Introduction to Modern Austrian Capital Theory. X, 196 pages. 1979.

Vol. 168: Convex Analysis and Mathematical Economics. Proceedings 1978. Edited by J. Kriens. V, 136 pages. 1979.

Vol. 169: A. Rapoport et al., Coalition Formation by Sophisticated Players. VII, 170 pages. 1979.

Vol. 170: A. E. Roth, Axiomatic Models of Bargaining. V, 121 pages. 1979.

Vol. 171: G. F. Newell, Approximate Behavior of Tandem Queues. XI, 410 pages. 1979.

Vol. 172: K. Neumann and U. Steinhardt, GERT Networks and the Time-Oriented Evaluation of Projects. 268 pages. 1979.

Vol. 173: S. Erlander, Optimal Spatial Interaction and the Gravity Model. VII, 107 pages. 1980.

Vol. 174: Extremal Methods and Systems Analysis. Edited by A. V. Fiacco and K. O. Kortanek. XI, 545 pages. 1980.

Vol. 175: S. K. Srinivasan and R. Subramanian, Probabilistic Analysis of Redundant Systems. VII, 356 pages. 1980.

Vol. 176: R. Färe, Laws of Diminishing Returns. VIII, 97 pages. 1980.

Vol. 177: Multiple Criteria Decision Making-Theory and Application. Proceedings, 1979. Edited by G. Fandel and T. Gal. XVI, 570 pages. 1980.

Vol. 178: M. N. Bhattacharyya, Comparison of Box-Jenkins and Bonn Monetary Model Prediction Performance. VII, 146 pages. 1980.

Vol. 179: Recent Results in Stochastic Programming. Proceedings, 1979. Edited by P. Kall and A. Prékopa. IX, 237 pages. 1980.

Vol. 180: J. F. Brotchie, J. W. Dickey and R. Sharpe, TOPAZ – General Planning Technique and its Applications at the Regional, Urban, and Facility Planning Levels. VII, 356 pages. 1980.

Vol. 181: H. D. Sherali and C. M. Shetty, Optimization with Disjunctive Constraints. VIII, 156 pages. 1980.

Vol. 182: J. Wolters, Stochastic Dynamic Properties of Linear Econometric Models. VIII, 154 pages. 1980.

Vol. 183: K. Schittkowski, Nonlinear Programming Codes. VIII, 242 pages. 1980.

Vol. 184: R. E. Burkard and U. Derigs, Assignment and Matching Problems: Solution Methods with FORTRAN-Programs. VIII, 148 pages. 1980.

Vol. 185: C. C. von Weizsäcker, Barriers to Entry. VI, 220 pages. 1980.

Vol. 186: Ch.-L. Hwang and K. Yoon, Multiple Attribute Decision Making – Methods and Applications. A State-of-the-Art-Survey. XI, 259 pages. 1981.

Vol. 187: W. Hock, K. Schittkowski, Test Examples for Nonlinear Programming Codes. V. 178 pages. 1981.

Vol. 188: D. Bös, Economic Theory of Public Enterprise. VII, 142 pages. 1981.

Vol. 189: A. P. Lüthi, Messung wirtschaftlicher Ungleichheit. IX, 287 pages. 1981.

Vol. 190: J. N. Morse, Organizations: Multiple Agents with Multiple Criteria. Proceedings, 1980. VI, 509 pages. 1981.

Vol. 191: H. R. Sneessens, Theory and Estimation of Macroeconomic Rationing Models. VII, 138 pages. 1981.

Vol. 192: H. J. Bierens: Robust Methods and Asymptotic Theory in Nonlinear Econometrics. IX, 198 pages. 1981.

Vol. 193: J. K. Sengupta, Optimal Decisions under Uncertainty. VII, 156 pages. 1981.

Vol. 194: R. W. Shephard, Cost and Production Functions. XI, 104 pages. 1981.

Vol. 195: H. W. Ursprung, Die elementare Katastrophentheorie. Eine Darstellung aus der Sicht der Ökonomie. VII, 332 pages. 1982.

Vol. 196: M. Nermuth, Information Structures in Economics. VIII, 236 pages. 1982.

Vol. 197: Integer Programming and Related Areas. A Classified Bibliography. 1978 – 1981. Edited by R. von Randow. XIV, 338 pages. 1982.

Vol. 198: P. Zweifel, Ein ökonomisches Modell des Arztverhaltens. XIX, 392 Seiten. 1982.

Vol. 199: Evaluating Mathematical Programming Techniques. Proceedings, 1981. Edited by J.M. Mulvey. XI, 379 pages. 1982.

Vol. 200: The Resource Sector in an Open Economy. Edited by H. Siebert. IX, 161 pages. 1984.

Vol. 201: P. M. C. de Boer, Price Effects in Input-Output-Relations: A Theoretical and Empirical Study for the Netherlands 1949–1967. X, 140 pages. 1982.

Vol. 202: U. Witt, J. Perske, SMS – A Program Package for Simulation and Gaming of Stochastic Market Processes and Learning Behavior. VII, 266 pages. 1982.

Vol. 203: Compilation of Input-Output Tables. Proceedings, 1981. Edited by J. V. Skolka. VII, 307 pages. 1982.

Vol. 204: K. C. Mosler, Entscheidungsregeln bei Risiko: Multivariate stochastische Dominanz. VII, 172 Seiten. 1982.

Vol. 205: R. Ramanathan, Introduction to the Theory of Economic Growth. IX, 347 pages. 1982.

Vol. 206: M. H. Karwan, V. Lotfi, J. Telgen, and S. Zionts, Redundancy in Mathematical Programming. VII, 286 pages. 1983.

Vol. 207: Y. Fujimori, Modern Analysis of Value Theory. X, 165 pages. 1982.

Vol. 208: Econometric Decision Models. Proceedings, 1981. Edited by J. Gruber. VI, 364 pages. 1983.

Vol. 209: Essays and Surveys on Multiple Criteria Decision Making. Proceedings, 1982. Edited by P. Hansen. VII, 441 pages. 1983.

Vol. 210: Technology, Organization and Economic Structure. Edited by R. Sato and M. J. Beckmann. VIII, 195 pages. 1983.

Vol. 211: P. van den Heuvel, The Stability of a Macroeconomic System with Quantity Constraints. VII, 169 pages. 1983.

Vol. 212: R. Sato and T. Nôno, Invariance Principles and the Structure of Technology. V, 94 pages. 1983.

Vol. 213: Aspiration Levels in Bargaining and Economic Decision Making. Proceedings, 1982. Edited by R. Tietz. VIII, 406 pages. 1983.

Vol. 214: M. Faber, H. Niemes und G. Stephan, Entropie, Umweltschutz und Rohstoffverbrauch. IX, 181 Seiten. 1983.

Vol. 215: Semi-Infinite Programming and Applications. Proceedings, 1981. Edited by A. V. Fiacco and K. O. Kortanek. XI, 322 pages. 1983.

Vol. 216: H. H. Müller, Fiscal Policies in a General Equilibrium Model with Persistent Unemployment. VI, 92 pages. 1983.

Vol. 217: Ch. Grootaert, The Relation Between Final Demand and Income Distribution. XIV, 105 pages. 1983.

Vol. 218: P. van Loon, A Dynamic Theory of the Firm: Production, Finance and Investment. VII, 191 pages. 1983.

Vol. 219: E. van Damme, Refinements of the Nash Equilibrium Concept. VI, 151 pages. 1983.

Vol. 220: M. Aoki, Notes on Economic Time Series Analysis: System Theoretic Perspectives. IX, 249 pages. 1983.

Vol. 221: S. Nakamura, An Inter-Industry Translog Model of Prices and Technical Change for the West German Economy. XIV, 290 pages. 1984.

Vol. 222: P. Meier, Energy Systems Analysis for Developing Countries. VI, 344 pages. 1984.

Vol. 223: W. Trockel, Market Demand. VIII, 205 pages. 1984.

Vol. 224: M. Kiy, Ein disaggregiertes Prognosesystem für die Bundesrepublik Deutschland. XVIII, 276 Seiten. 1984.

Vol. 225: T. R. von Ungern-Sternberg, Zur Analyse von Märkten mit unvollständiger Nachfragerinformation. IX, 125 Seiten. 1984

Vol. 226: Selected Topics in Operations Research and Mathematical Economics. Proceedings, 1983. Edited by G. Hammer and D. Pallaschke. IX, 478 pages. 1984.

Vol. 227: Risk and Capital. Proceedings, 1983. Edited by G. Bamberg and K. Spremann. VII, 306 pages. 1984.

Vol. 228: Nonlinear Models of Fluctuating Growth. Proceedings, 1983. Edited by R. M. Goodwin, M. Krüger and A. Vercelli. XVII, 277 pages. 1984.

Vol. 229: Interactive Decision Analysis. Proceedings, 1983. Edited by M. Grauer and A. P. Wierzbicki. VIII, 269 pages. 1984.

Vol. 230: Macro-Economic Planning with Conflicting Goals. Proceedings, 1982. Edited by M. Despontin, P. Nijkamp and J. Spronk. VI, 297 pages. 1984.

Vol. 231: G. F. Newell, The M/M/∞ Service System with Ranked Servers in Heavy Traffic. XI, 126 pages. 1984.

Vol. 232: L. Bauwens, Bayesian Full Information Analysis of Simultaneous Equation Models Using Integration by Monte Carlo. VI, 114 pages. 1984.

Vol. 233: G. Wagenhals, The World Copper Market. XI, 190 pages. 1984.

Vol. 234: B.C. Eaves, A Course in Triangulations for Solving Equations with Deformations. III, 302 pages. 1984.

Vol. 235: Stochastic Models in Reliability Theory. Proceedings, 1984. Edited by S. Osaki and Y. Hatoyama. VII, 212 pages. 1984.

Vol. 236: G. Gandolfo, P.C. Padoan, A Disequilibrium Model of Real and Financial Accumulation in an Open Economy. VI, 172 pages. 1984.

Vol. 237: Misspecification Analysis. Proceedings, 1983. Edited by T. K. Dijkstra. V, 129 pages. 1984.

Vol. 238: W. Domschke, A. Drexl, Location and Layout Planning. IV, 134 pages. 1985.

Vol. 239: Microeconomic Models of Housing Markets. Edited by K. Stahl. VII, 197 pages. 1985.

Vol. 240: Contributions to Operations Research. Proceedings, 1984. Edited by K. Neumann and D. Pallaschke. V, 190 pages. 1985.

Vol. 241: U. Wittmann, Das Konzept rationaler Preiserwartungen. XI, 310 Seiten. 1985.

Vol. 242: Decision Making with Multiple Objectives. Proceedings, 1984. Edited by Y. Y. Haimes and V. Chankong. XI, 571 pages. 1985.

Vol. 243: Integer Programming and Related Areas. A Classified Bibliography 1981–1984. Edited by R. von Randow. XX, 386 pages. 1985.

Vol. 244: Advances in Equilibrium Theory. Proceedings, 1984. Edited by C. D. Aliprantis, O. Burkinshaw and N. J. Rothman. II, 235 pages. 1985.

Vol. 245: J. E. M. Wilhelm, Arbitrage Theory. VII, 114 pages. 1985.

Vol. 246: P. W. Otter, Dynamic Feature Space Modelling, Filtering and Self-Tuning Control of Stochastic Systems. XIV, 177 pages. 1985.

Vol. 247: Optimization and Discrete Choice in Urban Systems. Proceedings, 1983. Edited by B. G. Hutchinson, P. Nijkamp and M. Batty. VI, 371 pages. 1985.

Vol. 248: Plural Rationality and Interactive Decision Processes. Proceedings, 1984. Edited by M. Grauer, M. Thompson and A.P. Wierzbicki. VI, 354 pages. 1985.

Vol. 249: Spatial Price Equilibrium: Advances in Theory, Computation and Application. Proceedings, 1984. Edited by P. T. Harker. VII, 277 pages. 1985.

Vol. 250: M. Roubens, Ph. Vincke, Preference Modelling. VIII, 94 pages. 1985.

Vol. 251: Input-Output Modeling. Proceedings, 1984. Edited by A. Smyshlyaev. VI, 261 pages. 1985.

Vol. 252: A. Birolini, On the Use of Stochastic Processes in Modeling Reliability Problems. VI, 105 pages. 1985.

Vol. 253: C. Withagen, Economic Theory and International Trade in Natural Exhaustible Resources. VI, 172 pages. 1985.

Vol. 254: S. Müller, Arbitrage Pricing of Contingent Claims. VIII, 151 pages. 1985.

Vol. 255: Nondifferentiable Optimization: Motivations and Applications. Proceedings, 1984. Edited by V. F. Demyanov and D. Pallaschke. VI, 350 pages. 1985.

Vol. 256: Convexity and Duality in Optimization. Proceedings, 1984. Edited by J. Ponstein. V, 142 pages. 1985.

Vol. 257: Dynamics of Macrosystems. Proceedings, 1984. Edited by J.-P. Aubin, D. Saari and K. Sigmund. VI, 280 pages. 1985.

Vol. 258: H. Funke, Eine allgemeine Theorie der Polypol- und Oligopolpreisbildung. III, 237 pages. 1985.

Vol. 259: Infinite Programming. Proceedings, 1984. Edited by E. J. Anderson and A. B. Philpott. XIV, 244 pages. 1985.

Vol. 260: H.-J. Kruse, Degeneracy Graphs and the Neighbourhood Problem. VIII, 128 pages. 1986.

Vol. 261: Th. R. Gulledge, Jr., N. K. Womer, The Economics of Made-to-Order Production. VI, 134 pages. 1986.

Vol. 262: H. U. Buhl, A Neo-Classical Theory of Distribution and Wealth. V, 146 pages. 1986.